ADVANCE PRAISE FOR *Rise and Shine*

"When you think of iconic and game-changing athletes in our sport of fastpitch softball, Monica Abbott immediately comes to mind. Her willingness to leave California and venture to the University of Tennessee set the collegiate landscape on fire. Her dedication to Team USA brought back numerous gold medals all while having a storybook professional career in Japan. Monica has set numerous records at every level of the game she's played. The name 'Monica Abbott' will be revered throughout the history of our sport—not just as an outstanding athlete, but an outstanding role model and person."

    —**Michele Smith**, ESPN analyst and two-time Olympic Gold Medalist

"Monica Abbott is one of the most impactful players we have ever seen in our collegiate program. She had a vision of where we were going. She had a bigger view of life beyond just herself. She impacted softball at the University of Tennessee, all the SEC, nationally, and internationally. *Rise and Shine: The Monica Abbott Story* offers insight into the talent, skills, and hard work required to achieve athletic greatness. More importantly, we see Monica's humility and her dedication to give to her sport and life. She is an inspiration to all of us."

    —**Joan Cronan**, women's athletic director Emeritus,
      University of Tennessee, Knoxville

"Monica's career illustrates the elusive accomplishment of dominance and longevity. Her will to be great and stay great has inspired generations of athletes, including myself. Competing against Monica in my playing career was a gift because each moment demanded an elite level of mental and physical stamina. Being challenged in that way is something I will always be grateful for."

    —**Lauren Chamberlain**, Women's Professional Fastpitch commissioner

RISE AND SHINE

RISE AND SHINE

THE MONICA ABBOTT STORY

MONICA ABBOTT *With Debby and Rob Schriver*

The University of Tennessee Press / Knoxville

A generous contribution from Linda Natiello Friedland in memory of
her mother, Isabella Hislop Tait Hunter Natiello (1911–1971), helped fund the
publication of this book. Isabella was born and raised in Edinburgh, Scotland,
and came to America at the age of nineteen. She instilled in her daughter
a love of books and reading.

Library of Congress Cataloging-in-Publication Data

Names: Abbott, Monica, 1985- author. | Schriver, Debby, other. | Schriver,
    Rob, other.
Title: Rise and shine : the Monica Abbott story / Monica Abbott, with Debby
    and Rob Schriver.
Description: First edition. | Knoxville : The University of Tennessee
    Press, [2023] | Summary: "This is an 'as-told-to' autobiography of
    University of Tennessee alumna Monica Abbott, who is a world-renowned
    professional softball pitcher in the National Professional Fastpitch
    league—indeed, the first female athlete in softball to sign a
    million-dollar contract. The narrative relates Abbott's rather humble
    beginnings, initially not even much interested in sports but finding
    herself captivated by softball. The story will serve as an inspiration
    for other athletes, especially girls and women, as they find their way
    into organized sports"—Provided by publisher.
Identifiers: LCCN 2023003324 (print) | LCCN 2023003325 (ebook) | ISBN
    9781621908319 (paperback : alk. paper) | ISBN 9781621908326 (pdf) | ISBN
    9781621908333 (Kindle edition)
Subjects: LCSH: Abbott, Monica, 1985- | Pitching (Softball)—United
    States—Biography. | Women softball players—United States—Biography. |
    University of Tennessee, Knoxville. Department of Athletics—History.
Classification: LCC GV881.4.P57 A33 2023 (print) | LCC GV881.4.P57
    (ebook) | DDC 796.357/8092 [B]—dc23/eng/20230126
LC record available at https://lccn.loc.gov/2023003324
LC ebook record available at https://lccn.loc.gov/2023003325

Cover photo credits: UT Athletics; USA Softball: Jade Hewitt; Toyota Red
Terriers; Wilson Ball Glove; Monica Abbott's personal collection.

This book is dedicated to all the moms out there empowering their daughters and not only believing but helping them make their biggest dreams come true, just like my mom, Julie, did.

This book is also dedicated to all the Girl Dads . . . fighting for their daughters to be the best version of themselves and instilling in them confidence to be the best they can be, no matter what the world is telling them, just like my dad, Bruce, did.

May we all never settle for anything less than our best.

CONTENTS

FOREWORD

Monica Abbott is beautifully unique, and I have never met anyone like her.

Among all the elite athletes I have interviewed and been around, she has always stood out because she is confident in the person she is and leads with a unique style that has always been inclusive of those around her.

I knew of Monica well before meeting her. She had been a big deal in high school and college at Tennessee. We became close when she was selected for the US Olympic team. At the time she was the youngest on the Olympic team, and I could immediately tell that she wanted to learn. She asked a lot of questions. She paid attention to others. She was always humble to understand we all needed to be better, and every day she wanted to know how she could be great.

Besides her immense talent, Monica understood there was more to greatness. We would go on walks and talk. Monica would tell me that she wanted to understand and to learn. She was unbelievably receptive to learning. The talent was there. It takes a lot to be the youngest on the Olympic team with so much experience and talent. I told her to just be herself. OWN who she was—and have an understanding of how those differences would work with a team full of women.

The humility was there. She has a ton of humility. She needed to learn about confidence—to balance the humility with confidence. She needed to hold a mirror up to see herself—to see how great she was. As she learned confidence, she learned to have that swag.

As I reflect back on our Olympic years, I remember that she was always out early to train. Monica and I were part of the few that were crazy enough to always be out there training with the sports performance coach. Monica's humility made her work ethic strong. She would work on her fielding. It was her one weakness. It's not easy for a tall left-handed pitcher to get low and handle a bunt. After seeing her in a game last year in Tokyo, I noticed that she has now made fielding another strength.

What makes Monica stand out is her heart. She has a huge one. She sees the world in a special way—wanting to make it better—not only in sport but outside of sport. To be Monica Abbott is to leave the world a better place. She is a different person. She told me things that I never would have thought about. It is easy to get caught up in the sport, but for Monica there is never a moment too big that shadows life outside sport.

The biggest impact she had on the softball world was her decision to go to the University of Tennessee. The New York Yankees had the house that Ruth built, and the SEC was the conference that Monica built. As the number-one recruit in the nation, her decision exploded that conference. Her decision was astonishing. First, a California native left the PAC -12 to go to Tennessee, and, second, she left the region to play for a team that had never seen an Oklahoma City. She put Tennessee on the map, took them to the World Series and to the finals against Arizona. She completely changed the college game.

And then she changed the game in Japan. There had been other Americans who played in Japan, but no one with the impact that she has had. She continues to help and lift up other players.

Monica understands expectations of her as a role model. She may not have seen herself as a superstar. She would say, "Why are they all chanting my name?" But she always understood that people wanted to be around her and accepted her role as a model for young people.

As a women's advocate, Monica has helped to reshape the image of beauty and strength. She is 6'3" tall and powerful. With great humility, Monica stares down her weaknesses and changes them into strengths. With determined confidence she will go down as one of the greatest pitchers and humans in the history of our sport.

I am buying this book for my sons because what she says impacts all of us. I can't wait to see and experience the next chapter in Monica Abbott's life.

JESSICA MENDOZA
ESPN Announcer
Stanford All-American
Two-time Olympic Medalist
Pro Fastpitch All Star and MVP

ACKNOWLEDGMENTS

I am so grateful to so many people who have helped to make this book possible. Over the course of my softball career I have had countless people that have impacted my life greatly. Some for a moment in time, some for a season, many are mentioned in this book, but it would be impossible to name them all.

I want to start by thanking my family: my mom, Julie, the very first catcher I ever had, and my dad, Bruce, who did a lot of the scorekeeping. Wow, am I grateful for you all and for the time invested to help me be successful. Sorry for all the dents in the car and missed pitches you found in the bushes, but wow—did we make some memories together. Mom, thank you for encouraging me and making time to catch for me in the beginning. You helped build a dream and a spirit of a determined attitude. Dad, thank you for challenging me and helping me figure out how to not just pitch, but to be smart about pitching, to have intention behind each pitch.

To my siblings, Jessica, Jared, Gina, and Bina: Thank you for being my rock, my competitive fire, and for being the someones I could count on. You all are still my first friends.

Thank you to Kenny Gardner the pitching coach that made it fun! and exciting! To Keith Berg, thank you for putting me in a position to be successful and continuing to find ways to challenge me as my skill level grew. To Jean Ashen, thank you for helping me realize how cool it is to be a female athlete. To Darren Jackson, for respecting my abilities in softball but challenging my athleticism in basketball. To the many friends, classmates, and teammates from NSHS, we pushed each other, we had fun, we laughed, and we grew up together. I'll always have that Viking Spirit.

To my Tennessee family: Thank you Ralph, thank you Karen, thank you Marty, thank you Michelle Granger. Thank you for taking a chance on a girl still trying to figure out where she fit in the world. Ralph, thank you for constantly challenging me and expecting my best, always. It wasn't easy, but it taught me how to pursue excellence. Karen, thank you for being patient with me and giving me a chance to figure out what a growth mindset meant to me. Marty, wow, that low rise changed my game. Thank you for believing in my rise ball, and therefore, for believing in me.

Thank you to my USA 2008 Teammates: Jessica Mendoza, Stacy Nuveman, thank you for taking a couple of rookies under your wing. Vicky Galindo, we had the time of our lives! To Natasha Watley, Tairia Flowers, Crystl Bustos, Caitlin Lowe, Laura Berg, Kelly Kretchman, Jennie Finch and Cat Osterman: we had some great times and memories on that 2008 tour; I'll cherish those times forever. You each individually taught me something about myself that helped me grow into the woman I am. Thank you.

Thank you to my Chicago Bandits staff and teammates. Daniele Zymkowitz, Mike Stuerwald, Jimmy Kolatis, Tammy Williams, Amber Patton, Vicky Galindo, Taylor Edwards, Kristin Butler, Jenna Grim, Brittany Cervantes, Roman Foore, Aaron Moore, Bill Sokolis, and so many more . . . I have so many happy memories in Chicago. We found ways to create the environment and atmosphere that we wanted, and we brought an entire community with us on that journey. It doesn't get better than that.

To my ScrapYard Dawgs family: It wasn't easy; we were challenged, but we persevered. Over and over we persevered and as Jimmy Kolatis said, "Don't poke the bear."

To my 2020/2021 Olympic teammates Ali Aguilar, Val Arioto, Haylie McCleney, Aubree Munro, Delaney Spaulding, Ally Carda, Keilani Ricketts, Coach Heather Tarr, Coach Dobson, Coach Berg: It wasn't easy. There was challenge after challenge. Thank you for making the journey just as fun and entertaining as the games and the competition we played. We did it in style, with grace and a laugh.

To Toyota Red Terriers: Fourteen years seems like a long time, but it went by quickly. Toyota softball made me learn to laugh at myself, to be okay with discomfort, to be challenged, and to be consistent. Kazuki Watanabe, Sachiko Itoh, Haruna Sakamoto, Satsuki Uemura, Yamane Sayuri, Sakura Miwa, Miu Goto, Yume Kirishi, Kyoko Ishikawa, Nana Iha, Yuki Kamata, Yuka Nakamura, Itsuhi Fukuda, Miyako Ikuhara, Aiko Nakamura : Ups and downs happen, but keep going. Never give up, and always give it your best!

To my husband, Jeff: You brought so much love and life to me. You have been my biggest supporter, accountability partner, and by my side every step of the way. You picked me up when I struggled getting through those tough moments, and I cherish our time and our life together.

And it is special that my Tennessee alma mater published this work. Scot Danforth, director of UT Press, and his staff of copyeditors, designers, and promoters have given my story form. Thanks to our readers for their insight and support.

Thanks to Beverly Buckley, for your dedication to women in sports and assisting as you did to give my book a bigger reach.

I want to thank the people that covered my career. The people that gave my story life in print, on TV, and in podcasts: Thank you for giving life to the story, John Devine, Mickey Dearstone, the Salinas *Californian, Monterey County Herald,* Aichi *Japan Times, Softball Magazine, Balls and Strikes Magazine, San Jose Mercury News,* and the *Knoxville News-Sentinel.*

I want to thank Rob and Debby Schriver for capturing my voice for this book. Many years ago when I finished playing at Tennessee, you said, one day I'll write a book about your story . . . and here we are all these years later. Thank you for being Lady Vol softball fans first, being advocates for women's sports, and for taking the time to listen and choosing my story to write about.

Of course, there are many others that I haven't been able to mention, but I will attempt to add a few more key people on my journey that have played a role in impacting and helping me develop as the person I am today: Karen Johns, Tara Brooks, Brian Davis, Pat Summitt, Philip Fulmer, Warren Wayland, Janice Bramers, Armando Barragan, Sara Fekete-Bailey, Shannon Doepking, Natalie Brock, Megan Smith, Stephanie Sayne, India Chiles, Lauren Mattox-Reeder, Paul and Stephanie Cater, the Sarmiento Family, Salinas Bobby Sox, Salinas Storm, Todd Leach, Pat Murphy, Sue Enquist, Kirk Walker, Dina Kwitt, Jade Hewitt, Don Deonatis Jr, Allison Parsell, Kirk Ihlenburg, Alan Jaeger, the Bowers, Julie Bartel, Michael McGarvey, Billie Jean King, Sara Pauly, Cheri Kemp, Holly Rowe, ESPN, MLB Network, NPF, NFCA, NCAA, sponsors Jaeger Sports and Wilson Sporting Goods, Fosters Freeze Salinas, Dana and Anjelicka Abbott, Jim and Teri Barnett, Andrea Kenney, CSUMB Softball, Fosters Freeze Santa Cruz, Salinas Girls Fastpitch, and the Community Foundation of Monterey County.

I'd like to give a special shout out to two that have since passed, but had their impact nonetheless: To my Grandparents Robert and Charlotte Abbott, thank you for being big parts of my life and teaching me about hard work and dedication early on. You both inspired me so much as a young child but even more as an adult. I still miss you.

Lastly, I want to give thanks to my one and only Lord and Savior. Without faith, I wouldn't have made it through those tough college days, without grace I wouldn't have made it through those tough days playing in Japan. I'm not perfect but knowing you are watching over me, guiding me, and giving me strength helps me keep going. I pray that I can continue to glorify your name in all that I do and that your light may shine through me for all that know and watch me. May they know that you live in me.

MONIE

ONE IN THE BEGINNING

It was an early warm Saturday spring morning, a great day for a softball tournament. It was about the fifth inning when the crowd started to build, lining the fence, packing the bleachers, and watching with anticipation as the thirteen-year-old pitcher fixed her eyes on the catcher. Tall for her age, Monica went into a coil at her waist, reached back to begin the circular motion, and released her pitch. The crowd erupted into cheers when Monica Abbott threw her record-setting twenty-one strikeouts—a perfect winning game. Who was this girl?

That was me, and to this day I love playing softball. But I wasn't always good at softball.

My earliest memories are of my parents growing the family business, Fosters Freeze, started by my grandparents. One of five kids, I have an older sister, younger brother, and two younger twin sisters. We had a really busy household, and now as an adult, I marvel at my parents' abilities to take care of us all and run a demanding restaurant business. We were a rowdy bunch—loud, little giants—always playing games. With a child in every age group, our home was the gathering place for the neighborhood. We played ball, freeze tag, four square, raced bikes around the block, and made up our own games. Indoors we played board and card games. I was always the one who got the games going.

Our grandparents had a pool, and we all loved playing there with our cousins and other kids. One time, while we were waiting for the adults to get ready so we could get in the pool, the older kids were swinging baseball bats. My sister grabbed a bat from the hands of my cousin Gavin, swung without looking around, and BAM! It hit me right in the eye. That was my introduction to softball, and what an introduction! I joined the other kids in ball games played in our street. We practiced in the street in front of our house. When cars came

On a family camping trip, Dad (Bruce) driving stroller with Jessica (*far right*) and Monica with her arm around Jared (*left*). Twins Bina and Gina get a free ride.

through, we called "timeout," and after they passed, "time in." We played hard, sweated, got dirty, and had so much fun. I love being outdoors.

When I was in first grade, my older sister, Jessica, came home from school with a Salinas Bobby Sox League flyer.* All her friends at school were playing, and she asked mom if she could play. Mom said, "I know that league because I played a couple of years in it. I am going to sign you up, and Monica, too." So I ended up playing on the team with Jessica. My parents' business sponsored the team, and it became a family affair. It was easy for mom to take us both to play at the same time. We were two years apart, so I was playing

---

* Salinas Bobby Sox is a girls' softball league open to all girls ages four to eighteen to learn and play fastpitch softball. There are no tryouts, and everyone plays. The league opened in 1970.

with older kids all the time. Jessica was strong, and she ended up being the shortstop, number-four hitter, and all-around All-Star. She was everyone's favorite player. Everyone wanted her on the team. But if they took Jessica, they had to have Monica. I guess I was always the tag-along. The problem with that was that in the beginning of my career, I was not very good. I was happier leading cheers in the dugout. I liked eating snacks and turning a foul ball in for candy. I was about everything going on but the actual game of softball. I played two innings in right field. It was mandatory for every player to get in the game.

One year Jessica was the All-Star on her team, and they needed a pitcher. My mom and my family, somehow, all decided to train Jessica to be the pitcher. She was already good at everything else—all of it. So, they decided, "Let's get Jessica a pitching lesson." We went out to the local rec field, where someone had recommended a coach named Kenny Gardner. Jessica got this pitching lesson, and my mom said, "Guess who gets to catch for Jessica? Monica has to catch for Jessica!" I was terrified. Literally. First off, I was not very good at softball. I played right field. I was there for snacks. I was there to chase foul balls so I could turn them in at the snack bar for licorice and lollipops. I enjoyed doing the monkey bars in the outfield. I was not really into softball. So when mom said, "We are going to get Jessica pitching lessons, and Monica, you are catching," I was so mad. I had to squat behind this plate in old, used catcher's gear for thirty minutes and catch. I had trouble putting the gear on. My knees hurt, and Jessica threw hard; it was scary. I was literally diving out of the way of the ball. Oops! Nope! Pick it up! I was the queen of stalling that day! Throwing it back. Again, diving out of the way. After the lesson, I was struggling out of the shin guards when Coach Gardner said, "Monica?" I looked up at him and had an expression on my face . . . WHAA-AT? "You don't like catching, do you?" No, this is awful! Here I was—I thought I was being sneaky, pretending to miss the ball. "Monica, you are a little tall. You're a lefty. I've heard you have played a bunch of other positions, but have you ever tried pitching?" I looked at him and said, "Nope. No, I haven't." Kenny Gardner said, "I think you should try pitching. I would love to give you a pitching lesson sometime."

We went home and forgot about it. I rode bikes with my friends. We played in the streets. A week later I went to my mom and asked, "Mom, can I have a pitching lesson? Remember that coach? He said I could be good at pitching. I really don't like playing right field anymore. The coach won't let me play shortstop. Can I try pitching? Can I just have a lesson? What about *me*, Mom?" And my mom looked at me and said, "No." She said, "Monica, no, we are not giving you a lesson." I asked her again the next day, and she said, "No." So, I asked her again the next day, and she said, "Monica, you don't even like softball. Do you really want to pitch?" I told her, "Yes, I want to try it. He said I could be good, Mom. Why not me? Can I get a lesson? Come on, Jessica got one." (I was playing the younger sister card here, hoping it would work since my other attempts had failed.)

My mom looked at me, and she literally gave me a laundry list of chores— chores nobody wanted to do—and said, "If you do all these things like vac- uum the car, mow the lawn, clean the bathroom, mop the kitchen floor, and clean out the junk drawer"—the kind that everyone has—"then we will give you a lesson." And I looked at my mom so excited and exclaimed, "Okay, deal!" My mom was testing me. How bad did I really want to do this? And she was thinking, "Maybe I'll get a bunch of chores out of her—things that I have not had time to do. I'll give her a lesson, and it will be over."

I did all the chores, and I got that lesson—that first pitching lesson. And I'll never forget after that first pitching lesson, I thought, "Oh my gosh, this is fun. Maybe I can be good at this. This coach thinks I could be. I got the lesson; now all I have to do is practice." That's when I started to create an af- ter-school practice routine. I came home from school after my first pitching lesson and said, "Mom, coach says I need to practice. Can we practice? Mom, can you play catch with me? I need to practice."

At that time, I was in fifth grade, and the twins were really young. So when I got home from school, they would go down for a nap, and my mom would practice with me. Every day when I got home, I put everything we needed out in the street: a bucket, a couple of softballs, a mitt, water for my mom, water for me, and a catcher's mask and shin guards for my mom. Mom would set a timer for thirty minutes. And that is how I created a practice routine. I set out that bucket literally every day after school for the 30 minutes. It was precious time with my mom, and I loved it! I was obviously still learning. I hit a lot of stuff. We lost a lot of balls, mostly to the bushes. If I missed her glove, my mom would make me chase it. She would say, "Nope, you're going to get it." Mom always said, "Don't throw the ball in the bushes, Monica. If you do, practice is over. We only have so many balls! Your thirty minutes will be up if you lose the ball in the bushes. Once it goes in there, it is hard to get it out." When she jumped away, my pitches became weapons, denting the car door, the house, and other targets. Sometimes they hit the brick planter and bounced back, and I thanked my lucky stars!

Mom wore all the gear, the catcher mask and catcher knee guards. She was tall like me, about 5'10." This practice was great, and I was improving. Because my mom made me chase after the wild pitches myself, I learned to throw the ball more accurately. She always repeated what the coach said: "You have to follow through, point!" After a while, I started pitching faster —a lot faster. I was pitching so much faster that my mom was screaming "Aaaaack!" each time she caught the ball. And later she started screaming "Aaaaack!" twice —once before the ball got there upon release or in anticipation, and then "Aaaaack!" again when she closed her eyes and the ball hit in her glove.

So, I started looking for another catcher. I tried my dad, but he wore glasses, and one day I broke his glasses while pitching to him. After that my dad stuck with his umpiring and scorekeeping duties at the Bobby Sox League games we played. Around this time, maybe a year later, I started taking monthly pitching lessons from Kenny Gardner.

That same year, our teacher told us we would each be assigned a state to research and report on for class. I was excited, hoping that I would get Arizona, Nevada, or Colorado. So, when my teacher assigned me Georgia for my report, I was disappointed. I didn't know anything about that part of the country and really had no interest in Georgia. But I learned that that year—1996—Atlanta was hosting the Olympics! Softball was an Olympic sport! I devoured every bit of information I could about Georgia, and I earned an A+ on that report. That's when I decided that I would be an Olympian. I wrote that in my report! My dream was written in the stars . . . or my fifth grade state report.

Those were fun years playing sports with my family. I kept a scrapbook of

"I knew Monica was special when she was pulled up to play travel ball with her older sister on a road trip to Colorado. She got to pitch in a game and struck out the first two people she faced. The opposing coach was upset with his own player for striking out. He went out on the field furious that his fourteen-year-old player struck out to a twelve-year-old."

Bruce Abbott, Monica's father

pictures from that time—black and white pictures, fifth and sixth grade. I swam and played volleyball and basketball, but as I grew older and got better at pitching, I stepped away from swimming and volleyball to devote more time to softball. My parents never forced me to play softball, but I wanted to pitch. I continued to play basketball even through high school in the off season.

Before long, the time came to move from the Bobby Sox League to the Salinas Storm Club Team.* It was tough telling the coach at the recreation league that I was leaving that team. I was scared, but my parents made me tell him. That was an important part of growing up, I guess. I was in the age twelve and under group of Salinas Storm, and my sister was in the fourteen and under. One time my sister's team had a tournament scheduled in Colorado, and because I was her sister, they brought me up to play in her age group. My family was going to drive there to give us a little vacation trip around softball. (We actually had a vacation! That didn't always happen.) Well, at the game our team was behind and not doing very well. The coach put me in, and here I was, the younger kid going up to bat. I had a hit! I was so excited that I just began waving my arms and cheering. The coach called to me, "Monica! Monica! Run to the base!" Two players on base scored. If I hadn't been so excited about getting a hit, I probably could have run all the way to home for a home run.

And that is how I started to become a good softball player. That's when I started to get hits—THE HIT! I started to move from right field. I spent a short time at shortstop and then second base, because I had a good arm. And then they realized I was left-handed, so I moved to first base and later started pitching. For some reason when I was growing up, being a left-handed pitcher was a rarity. Even when I was in college, there were very few left-handed pitchers. Now there are a ton everywhere! My grandma and my dad talk about this in my family. The lefty gene is supposed to skip generations—it is a recessive gene. In my family for some reason, it affects the mom-son-mom-son line and has for five generations. My dad is a lefty, and

*Salinas Storm is a part of Salinas Girls Fastpitch Inc., a nonprofit organization. Salinas Storm was established in 1992. The mission is to create a positive, competitive, supportive learning environment to build well-rounded athletes

14U Softball nationals, Monica is pitching for the Salinas Storm travel ball team.

of the five kids in our family, I am the only one who is left-handed. My dad's mom, my grandma, is left-handed, and she had all sons, and only one of them was left-handed. My grandma used to tell me stories about how they would try to switch her left-handedness growing up: she got into trouble for using her left hand in school. This also happened to my dad when he was in school, but my grandmother would not let them force him to be right-handed. Even though I faced similar challenges playing tennis, volleyball, golf, and in other random, everyday ways, being left-handed became an asset for me in softball. In the world there are fewer left-handed people, and so the world, in many ways, is set up from a right-handed perspective. When they are young, kids like to mimic to learn. Left-handers can't mimic; when we try, we become klutzy. Instead of mimicking, we have to mirror. In softball the majority of players are right-handed, but from the pitcher's mound a lefty gives a different perspective to the hitter. This can give lefties an advantage on the mound, because they have a natural spin or curve on the ball that a right-handed pitcher can't pull off.

As a small child, I found fun in sports. As I grew, sports became a means for me to grow confidence. I was always tall for my age, somewhat clumsy, and what some would call a "late bloomer." What other kids say can sting. I was quiet, not quite sure of myself except on the ball field. I knew that I was a good pitcher. I knew that I had discovered my niche. Playing softball gave me a way to escape, have fun, interact with other kids on a level playing field, and excel because of my build, physical abilities, and attitude. Sports created a classroom where I could learn more than softball, and every step gave me the confidence to be a successful, happy woman.

TWO THE VIKINGS, PROUD AND TOUGH

Salinas, California, has a number of public high schools. Our family's Fosters Freeze was just across the street from Salinas High School, which our family had attended for generations. So when our neighborhood was rezoned and I learned that I would be attending North Salinas High School, initially I was sad. This school was farther away, and I didn't know much about it. I was apprehensive, but I was also excited.

On my first day as a student at North Salinas High School, I met Jean Ashen, the athletic director and volleyball coach. I thought, "Oh my God, there is another woman who is tall like me!" I thought that was so cool. Coach Ashen invited me to play volleyball, and I did for a brief time. I was drawn more to basketball as an addition to softball, though. I had started playing in elementary school, and I played through middle school, so it only made sense for me to keep playing. I really liked it because it got me in great shape for softball. A lot of my friends played, too, so there was a social bonus of making friends with people who played basketball but didn't play softball. I was a double-double kid in high school. That means double figures in scoring and rebounding. Most of the people on our team were five foot five or shorter, but one other player was also tall, and we were called the "twin towers." Our basketball team was good.

Playing basketball was perfect timing because during the basketball season—November, December, January—I really didn't play a lot of softball. I took one pitching lesson a month just to maintain, and I remember Coach Gardner would

> "I knew Monica was an elite athlete the first day she was at school. The first year in PE class, I said to myself, 'Please play a sport.'"
>
> Jean Ashen, athletic director, North Salinas High School

Monica was a standout basketball player for the North Salinas Vikings basketball team. Here Monica (#25) posts up, waiting for a pass in the paint. She was known for a drop step move and a left-handed hook shot.

get so upset with me. He would say, "Monica, you haven't been practicing. I can tell!" He was right. I was playing basketball.

I loved sports, but I also participated in other extracurricular activities. I had a part-time job at Fosters Freeze, and I attended Regional Occupational Program (ROP), where we learned trades like woodworking, metalworking, and flower arranging. Thinking that I might want to be a physical therapist someday, I chose to study physical therapy. I also took sewing and learned how to make clothes. My mom is really big on sewing, so I already knew how to sew a little bit; I made pajama pants and pillows, and then for a group project, my friend and I made her prom dress. We got patterns, and we had to adjust the patterns to her size. It came out looking really good. I also sang alto in the chorus and played piano for twelve years.

I wasn't necessarily the smartest person, but I did all my homework. I did not do well on the SAT and ACT tests, but my GPA was good. Because I did all my homework, my ranking in the class was high my junior year. Teachers said that I needed to be in advanced placement (AP) classes, so they put me in AP English, calculus, and other hard classes. The moral of this story is that I ended up being in the National Honor Society and ranked eighth in my class because I did my homework—not because I got smarter. I did what was assigned to me; my job, so to speak. That is what made me successful in the classroom. I did my homework and paid attention.

When I go back to what was my social group, I didn't really have a clique that I hung out with. My social group was all over the board. I was in classes with the nerds; I played sports with all the athletes; and I was with the artsy people in all my elective classes. One of my best friends from elementary school wasn't sporty at all. Her family owned a bakery. She and I would just go from group to group and hang out with people. And then I had a younger brother who played sports, too, so I knew his friends. I was very much a social person. I was always talking in class, and teachers would get mad at me. Even to this day, I am that person who initiates fun: I was never the person who got invited to play or go roller skating with friends; I was the person doing the inviting.

Through all of this, I saw my parents working hard, even on weekends and nights. I witnessed their commitment to their work when they opened a second Fosters Freeze restaurant. Because of them, I was able to work part time, go to school, and play softball. I did homework at a table while they ran the business. I remember working my 6:00–9:00 shift and going to sleep in the car while my mom closed the restaurant at 11:00. And the part-time work I did there enabled me to pay for pitching lessons. In high school when we were beginning to set life goals for ourselves, I kept quiet when other kids declared they would never work in the fast-food business. Knowing how our family business supported my family and our goals, I wore my Fosters Freeze hat with pride.

By the time I was in high school, my older sister, Jessica, had finished high school, my brother, Jared, was a freshman, and my youngest twin sisters, Gina and Bina, were in elementary school. Everyone was playing sports, and schedules were tight. Everything was prioritized around softball at the time. After I got my driver's license, I began driving to school in my family's diesel Suburban. It was so loud—look out, here come the Abbotts! Sometimes I would take my siblings to their practices after school. A lot of times we would wait for each other; other times, I would go home and then come back

Youth softball collage from Monica's high school cultural heritage project. In the center you can see Mom (Julie) with older sister Jessica (*right*) and Monica (*left*).

later to pick them up. I think all of us watching out for each other not only kept us close, but helped my parents, too.

In the midst of all this, there were parts of high school that scared me just a little bit. Like many American high schools, North Salinas High School had its issues. There were drugs—not just marijuana but other hard drugs. I remember being on a high school basketball game trip, and a friend of mine was sitting with me on the bus. She was older than I was. She just started confiding in me: "I am high right now. I took a drug. I have to tell somebody. If something happens to me, make sure you tell. If a paramedic comes, be sure to tell them what I took. Make sure they know, but don't tell anyone else." Whoa! I was fifteen and totally naïve, and here was this girl, my friend, trusting me to do the right thing if something were to happen. In the same way, my friends would warn me: "But you—don't ever do this, Monica. Don't ever do something like this. You are too good to do something like this. Don't do what I did. Just know you shouldn't be doing this. You've got to make it."

When those sorts of things occurred, it was a reality check. On the inside I was thinking: "Holy moly, holy cow. This is bad. Why are they doing that? She doesn't need to be doing that. This is crazy." It also reminded me, "Hey, I need to be focused on what I want, otherwise I could easily go down. Accessibility is there if I want that. And I could easily go down that path." I think the violence and drug culture centered me and made me more focused. And then obviously as I got a little bit older, people started to protect me from it, too. They took care of their own. As I got older, the girls would say, "I did it, Monica, but you can't do it. We need you to make it. You can't come to this party. Don't you have softball practice?"

It was that kind of community.

I've seen people going down hard paths, being influenced by other people, and not making good choices. I've seen addiction and alcoholism. I've seen the violence and the fighting. I've seen the remnants of people. I've seen families whose brother or cousin was in a gang, and the entire family became victims of it. I do think when things are hitting hard, it's tough to be the sheltered one sometimes. It's tough to be the one who always has to say "No," being the one people are protecting, or just seeing some of that damage that people on a bad path are doing to themselves. I have seen that up close and personally and the effects that it has on the people that are close to you. Seeing it is so hard—especially as a teenager.

In my case, softball was there. Violence and troubles of the school forced me to focus more on softball. I knew the softball field, and practice with Coach Berg, was a safe space. No one was judging me there. I didn't have to explain what I saw or worry about how to respond. I could dive into that space and use it as an escape. In many ways, I think I just didn't have any other choice.

Softball was my comfort zone and a way out. It was my way out, and I knew that. It was just a matter of where I wanted to go. And I think other people saw that, too. People started saying, "Oh, my gosh, she's good. Monica is legit." They were seeing the newspapers. Everyone in the school knew. Everyone in the community knew. People weren't just encouraging me—they were becoming mother hens to make sure I didn't do something dumb.

I can say that my basketball coach, Darren Jackson, did that really well. I wanted him to be my coach because he understood the discipline needed to be a successful athlete. He knew softball was my passion. That's where I was going to go. He also knew I had opportunity in basketball, so he planted that seed when he could as well. He was a great person who protected me. He would say: "Monica, you don't need to hang out with that group. It's them and their drama. Don't go their way. You don't need them in your life. Focus on what you do. Do your softball. Don't get caught up in the drama. Don't get caught up in all the partying, the drugs, the boys. That time will come for you. Focus on what you need to do. Come hang out with me. Come be my co-pilot on the road trips. Stay out of the other stuff."

I never felt the weight of expectations or pressure to win from others in my high school. Everyone was so supportive. North Salinas High boasted a number of other athletes in different sports that successfully went on to college and to play professional. I feel like it was more of a sense of pride and joy for the community than, "Oh, you've got to win." They would say, "We can't wait to watch you play. Hope you get in the newspaper tomorrow." Even to this day when they see me, North Salinas High School alumni are saying, "Go Monica, go Vikings!" Community support isn't what created pressure. I was the one who wanted to win. I was pretty hard on myself. I played a lot of softball in high school—twenty-five games in spring season alone. During the fall I played for the club softball team, the Salinas Storm. Looking back now, I see that people got really excited to play against me in high school. They would say, "We are playing Monica Abbott today." Even Notre Dame,

Beloved basketball coach Darren Jackson with star player, Monica, before a Vikings game.

our rival, would always play better against us because they were excited to play me. We had some epic battles.

I always think that's kind of cool about North High. My high school itself had a blue-collar mentality. We weren't the nicest, prettiest high school around. We didn't have the nicest softball field, either—in fact, it had a grass infield. It had massive holes. Nobody wanted to play softball at North Salinas High School, because our field was terrible. But my junior year we organized a workday to change the infield to dirt. That was the thing about North High—there were a lot of working-class people that were just hustling. We were all people who did not have a lot of opportunities set up for us, but doors were opened, and we persevered almost to a fault. We all just kept going. A door opened, and we went for it. In a sense, our mentality was, "Why not us? I can do it just as well."

Our perseverance really gave a lot of pride to our school and to the community. These days I probably don't remember half the people I went to high school with. But on this past Saturday night we went to a restaurant in downtown Salinas, and five people said, "Oh my gosh, you are Monica Abbott. I went to high school with you. We love you. You have gotten so good."

To this day, there is so much pride from someone making it out of North High—someone who made it from that school. That wasn't a common thing. Most of the people went to a junior college or went into a trade—metal shop, wood shop, hair salon. People went to colleges; don't get me wrong. People went four years to school. But someone who made it athletically or made it in a positive way like that—it generated a lot of pride for North High and the people who graduated from it.

North Salinas High is not necessarily one of those schools that has a good softball team or a good football team every single year. But it is a school that puts out some surprisingly phenomenal athletes. We always say that for some reason in North Salinas High we have athletes that go on to be great. There are not a lot of us, but there is a strong handful. Alvin and Calvin Harrison were 100- and 200-meter sprinters. They went to the 1996 and 2000 Olympic Games, and both were gold medalists. And then there were Ronnie Lott, who played for the 49ers, and Carl Nix Jr., a seven-time all-pro offensive lineman, who played for the Dolphins. He and I are exactly the same age.

To this day, North Salinas High takes pride in these athletes and others who made it out. Salinas is a small town with deep, genuine pride. My parents' restaurant downtown has pictures of me. I came back a couple of years ago to a pizza place we used to go to, and they said, "You don't have to pay. It's on us. We just love everything you do. Our daughters play softball now." So then I went back with a picture for them to put up in their store. I grew up in a sweet spot. I always say that. Today everyone is on social media, but I grew up in a sweet spot of press because the newspaper was still being delivered. Everyone's parents got the newspaper. They saw our sports stories. And I think that's kind of cool too.

Home games in high school were always exciting. Anytime there was a game, I would wear my hair in two French braids down. I would wake up early and get my hair done before I went to school. And everybody would comment, "Oh, you have a game today, your hair is braided."

Walking through the halls of high school we were nervous all day, and we got to leave sixth period early. Games were always right after school at four o'clock or sometimes four thirty. Our team would get dressed in our uniforms before school was out and go back to class in our uniforms. Sometimes our athletic director, Jean Ashen, would stop us in the halls and say, "You guys are still supposed to be in class." And we said, "But we have to get a snack before the game." She would laugh and give us a hard time. The students weren't the only ones who got excited; the staff at the school got into it too. One of the janitors called me "Special K" because K is the symbol for strikeout. When I left class to go get ready—"Okay, I've got to get ready for my game!"—my teacher would look at the class and say, "Well, if you can throw a fastball as hard as Monica, you can leave early too." They would let the softball team out fifteen minutes early so we could go get ready. It was always really fun. They kept our equipment in this tiny closet, so we would have to drag it all the way to the field. (We took care of the field ourselves, and that's one reason it wasn't very good. We didn't know how to do it.)

> "There was a lot of interest and support for Monica in the community—and still is. They had a Monica Abbott Day this year."
>
> Bruce Abbott, Monica's father

My grandmother came to every single softball game—home and away. My grandma was a big supporter of my games and me. She had a kind of outlandish personality—very big personality. She had a huge laugh. "Monica, why'd you walk that batter?" She would say stuff like that. Or after a tough loss, she would say, "Monica, you can't win them all." Or she would say, "This is why you play, so you can come back tomorrow and win." She was super encouraging and very real. She would say something like, "Ahhh, I hate losing. We're going to have to win tomorrow." Everybody knew she was my grandma. She had bright white hair and bedazzled glasses. My mom and dad came to almost every game, too, depending on work and what the other kids were doing. When he came, my dad did the scorekeeping.

During the big games, everyone was really nervous. We'd say, "Are you nervous? Yes, I'm nervous! Are you nervous? Who's nervous? Everybody's nervous. Don't ask me!" When we were nervous, we yelled and cheered more. And I was a nervous Gatorade drinker, which was kind of bad because there were no bathrooms at the field. We had to run to the locker room to go to the bathroom. I think that is what happens in softball, even now. We get this nervous energy, so we come up with some funny stuff to say or cheer. We come up with things that are fun to do as a group.

The games were pretty intense. People would line the fence to watch.

There was a walkway next to the field that led from the classrooms to the neighborhood behind our school, and people would sit in that walkway to watch the games, too. We had a lot of coverage by the newspaper. And a lot of those epic games were definitely battles. We often played extra-inning games—ten, twelve, or fourteen—with our rival, Notre Dame. When I say North High wasn't very good, I mean that our offense wasn't very good. We lost games because there would be an overthrow in extra innings. We couldn't hit. I would strike out eighteen and lose the game, while the other pitcher would strike out twelve.

At that time, I really struggled to find a catcher for practice. My mom had been catching for me forever. Keith Berg was coaching his daughter, who was my age and on a different team. His daughter was a catcher. So, we teamed up and worked together. When his daughter stopped playing softball, Coach Berg continued to coach me. I was throwing really hard for a high school pitcher at that time. I was throwing more than sixty-five miles per hour. I had power.

But reality is reality; it is hard to put expectations on a team or yourself when you look at your home softball field and it has a grass infield. When your biggest rival is recruiting all these high school superstars, and you have a five foot two shortstop, yes, you want to win. You are going to do everything in your power to win.

THREE   THE PITCH THAT CHANGED MY LIFE

Going into the season my freshman year in high school, I was throwing a screwball and a really good curveball. I also had kind of a changeup—but not so great. At one pitching lesson Coach Gardner said, "You are going to high school, and now you can't really use a fastball anymore to locate a pitch. You have a good curveball; you have a screwball. What you need is something up or down. You are going to play with bigger hitters. They have some good pitchers at North Salinas High School. If you want to make the varsity team, you need to have another pitch." He continued, "I want to teach you how to throw a rise ball. You need one pitch that is going to get people out for you, and it can't be in or out. It has to be up or down." Coach Gardner said that all elite pitchers, anybody that is top level, had multiple pitches, but typically one pitch, usually the rise or drop, is more natural to them based on their body, their mechanics, and just how they throw in general. I throw both. My drop ball is good, but it is not at the level of my rise ball. Drop ball pitchers can throw a rise, but it usually isn't at the level of their drop.*

So, Coach Gardner taught me how to throw the rise ball. And it wasn't anything dramatic or mind blowing. He showed me a grip, and I did some drills with it. And then he threw it. In pitching lessons he would throw, and then I would try to copy him—mirror him. This visual way of teaching through imitation really helped me, especially at a young age. Now that I am older, I can be told what to do, and I am a lot better at it.

It took me about a month to learn to throw the rise ball. I started practicing, and it took off. My coach also worked with me doing the drop ball to figure out which pitch was better for me. Once we learned that I had a knack

*In or out and up or down refer to movement of the softball within the batter's strike zone over home plate.

Monica's long-time pitching coach Kenny Gardner after the high school championship game. Gardner started working with Monica when she was 12 years old.

for the rise ball, we just went all in on it. When I started playing high school softball, I was throwing the rise ball with just one problem: I couldn't control it. These pitches would start really low at the knees and then break the backstop (the fence or structure behind home plate)—super high, really fast, and no one could catch it. I had no control over it. Coach Gardner helped me learn how to control it and adjust my grips and release points so it would flow out of my hand better. I remember when I first started practicing it a lot, I could tell which ones were breaking sharply: the ball would come to the plate, and it was almost like it exploded up, extremely high through the strike zone. By the time it got to the catcher, they had to move their glove from their belly button back over their head to try to catch it.

You do have to be able to throw fast for a rise, but it helps. You have to have good mechanics to be able to throw a rise, especially at the end of your pitch, for it to truly rise. If you don't, it just looks like a high fastball instead of having a breaking point and going up. When you throw faster, you are able to get more revolutions right in the ball. Those revolutions power the spin up, so it becomes a sharper pitch when you throw faster. Throwing slower results in a kind of floating rise—really slow—and that is why they say you have to have speed. Otherwise, hitters can tell that the ball is going up, and anticipating the break, they can hit the ball because it is slow.

At the time when I was in high school, pitchers didn't really throw the rise. The game has evolved now, and most pitchers have a rise or a drop. You usually have one or the other. You don't have both. If you were going to college to pitch, you had a rise, a drop ball or a changeup that was good. That's what got you to college.

> **"With all of her strikeouts, I only ever saw one home run hit off of her. And I have to think that was lucky."**
>
> Kenny Gardner,
> pitching coach

When I was in high school, I was building my skills, sharpening my pitch, and learning more about the game. The catcher would call pitches, and then when Keith Berg became the coach my junior year, he called pitches because he knew me and the catcher. Sometimes when we were playing a weaker team, and we were winning by a lot, he would let us call the game. He wouldn't call at all. He would say: "Okay, you guys are winning 3–0, so go for it. If you get into trouble, I'm going to come back out." He was trying to teach us, and he sometimes even had me call pitches for one of our other pitchers when we were playing and I wasn't pitching. When we were winning by a few runs, he would let me call or talk me through it. Coach Berg was very empowering and pushed me to take the initiative.

I threw curveballs and rise balls. It depended on the hitter and the situation. I would throw low in the zone for a strike with a screw in the outside corner—nice and low. And then I would just throw two rise balls, and the hitter would strike out. Or they would foul one off and then strike out. Or I would do the opposite. If the hitter was really good, I would maybe start with two rise balls. If the hitter was good and could foul it off, let her foul it once, twice, then throw one nice and low, and see if I could get a strikeout.

When I say the rise ball changed my life, I really do mean that. I was living in a small northern California farming town, and I was working fast food for my family. Everyone in my family either went to junior college or went straight into the family business. Why was the rise ball so important to me? Late in my freshman year because of the rise ball, I had a real sense of going on to college softball. Colleges had already learned about me. Back in middle school when I pitched that twenty-one-strikeout game—which is the maximum number of strikeouts you can have in a game—I sent shockwaves through the softball world. But to me it was a 1–0 game, and we were just trying to win to qualify for nationals. At that time, I received recruiting letters from schools like UCLA, saying, "Who is this kid?" (It was the only kind of communication NCAA rules allowed.) I almost didn't realize that was anything to pay attention to. I just thought, "Yeah, right. This is a joke. They don't know me." So I never really thought about it. But once I started to get good at the rise ball during my freshman year of high school, I was striking people out. I made varsity. I had a rise ball now . . . whoa! I could go to college to play softball.

I jumped probably three levels just by being able to throw the rise ball. I went from people saying that I could be a good softball player to people saying, "Holy cow! We want to recruit you to college." The rise opened the door. That's the reason I made varsity as a freshman. At the time there were pitchers who threw the ball hard, and there were pitchers that threw a screwball and a curveball. But having a rise ball, having a pitch that was a game changer, separated me from other people. Suddenly I could throw literally 80 percent rise balls in a game. In the grand scheme of things, the rise ball is a unique pitch in softball, and it's a pitch that softball is known for. A lot of people throw it, but a lot of people don't throw it well. But when I learned it, I had a knack for it. I started throwing this rise ball and it just—WHOOF—took off.

And for about three months I had zero control of it, so I didn't really throw it that much. Coach Gardner said, "Well, if we can't get control of this rise ball, let's see if we can make it an off speed. Let's try to do something else on it and see if that helps you—and see if that can be a pitch for you." He adjusted my grip and had me tuck a finger on my rise ball, which was unheard of. This is what people throw for an off speed—to make the pitch a little bit slower, though not quite as slow as a changeup. I said, "Okay, let's try it. Let's do it." I threw it. And instead of being slow, it was just as fast, but it came under control. I tucked my finger on the ball, and all of a sudden, I was able to control it and not throw it over the catcher's head every minute. It was still breaking really well, and we pulled out a gun, and it's still at whatever speed it was I was throwing at the time, sixty-three, sixty-four, sixty-five mph. I'm still throwing it that fast. All of a sudden, holy cow, this is my grip!

So, I tucked a finger, and that is how I learned to control the rise ball. We started working on the spin and the break. Can we get it to where it breaks closer to home plate? It jumps a lot. And then fast forward two years into high school, and players were saying, "We know you are throwing a rise ball; we can see your finger tucked on the rise ball. We can see your grip." So, in a weird way, I ended up making it better. My coach told me, "Monica, it doesn't matter. If you can throw a pitch that they know is coming, and they are still going to swing and miss, then you know it's a great pitch. Your biggest challenge is to tell the hitter what you are throwing and make them swing and miss on it."

So, that became the philosophy. Okay, they know the rise ball is coming, and I'm going to throw it anyway. I'm going to get you out on it. Coach Berg was really great about this during our summer ball practices when we had the more elite-level players. I would go up; I would pitch in a practice and have the hitter call out the pitch I was throwing. We would give them choices of two pitches. The hitter would call out, or I would tell them what pitch I was going to throw. I would stand on the mound and say, "Okay, rise ball." And they would try to hit it or not hit it. Is it a strike or is it a ball? We worked counts that way. This made my pitch a lot better. This exercise was teaching me how to throw it through the zone and create really good sharp breaks and angles on it. And then all of a sudden, I was recruited by every school in the country. I had a rise ball now. I could go to college.

I was invited to the junior national team for Team USA. I played on the junior national team my senior year in high school. We went to Mexico for the Pan American Games—the junior world championships. I was one of the youngest players. I was a senior in high school throwing sixty-five mph and a rise ball. I have to give credit to Coach Berg for pushing me in that direction and for his motivating coaching style. He would say things like, "Awhhhh— it's a plane! It's a jet, 747 straight up! You've got the ball coming up. Give me the unhittable rise ball through the zone." He would say all these amazing things that would just pump me up and make me want to repeat it. But then he always found ways to challenge the entire team and me in practice. This made everybody better.

I learned that I could throw an amazing pitch. I wanted to make it not only good, but great. That really opened so many doors and opportunities for me. And when those doors opened, I ran through them and never looked back.

FOUR THE SHOCK HEARD AROUND THE SOFTBALL WORLD

In travel ball there was a point when my coach would say, "Wow, you are the number one recruit in the country right now!" And then he would say, "Some of these recruiters are saying you are not the number one recruit right now; this other girl is." I wasn't really tuned into comparisons of me on a national level. I didn't even know there was a ranking!

College wasn't emphasized at my high school, but it was assumed that everyone would go to the junior college in the area. Then maybe you go to another college after that. But it was emphasized to me by my parents that if I wanted to go to college to play softball, I had to have a full ride to go. My parents told me, "If you are going to go to college, you are going to have to get a full scholarship." That was embedded in me. There was no partial. It was all in or don't go, because we had five kids and they were all doing sports and all playing club ball.

Late in my high school freshman year because of the rise ball, I developed a desire to go on to college softball. In July of my sophomore year recruiting opened up, and I received fifty pieces of mail every day for six months. That is when the possibility of college started to feel real. I also received two or three basketball scholarship offers from colleges in the region where I lived, mostly because I only played in high school, so if they didn't come to the high school game, they never saw me. Colleges weren't allowed to talk to me yet, so at first, I just got letters.

Once I started getting those letters, I saw that college provided a way for me to get closer to my Olympic dream. I think my dream was always to be an Olympian, and college softball could bring me one step closer. College would be awesome; holy cow, I didn't even know this opportunity existed! When I was growing up, we didn't have cable TV. We got three channels with an antenna, so I didn't watch college or professional softball, or the Olympics. I went to the library and checked out a book or I learned about it at school. I went to one major league baseball game when I was probably in eighth grade with my aunt. The athletes that I knew were the athletes that were a couple of years older than I was, the athletes in my county area, or the athletes we played in travel ball in places like Los Angeles. That's what I knew.

My freshman year in high school we made nationals in travel ball. We went to Dallas, Texas, and then all of a sudden there were college coaches watching me. That's when I realized, "Oh my gosh, they are actually here!" My parents overheard conversations between the scouting coaches in the stands. They loved hearing the college coaches talking at the games in the background. They would say, "Nobody knows I'm your parent. They don't know I'm your mom. And they are talking about you. And I'm thinking, 'That's my daughter!'" And I would just say, "Can I have a Gatorade?" I was always trying to get her to bring me Gatorade.

Our team did really well in Dallas and played in the top five. I think we came in fourth in nationals, which is awesome considering that our town wasn't big. I pitched a ton, I hit, and I did great. We had a good tournament, went home, and everyone was happy because we played so well. I wasn't the only one being recruited; other people on my team were, too. Coaches came because they heard about me, but they were watching other players as well. I wasn't leaning toward any specific college. At this point I made a choice not to make a choice—to keep doing what I had been doing. Sometimes it's the best choice to make.

I got that first "who are you" letter from UCLA after I threw that twenty-one-strikeout, perfect game. And then nothing happened. I went on to high school, and then in my sophomore year, the letters started coming. I started getting mail almost nonstop from every college in the nation. I got a ton of mail. Soon other people on my team were receiving letters, too. Our team started to get better because they realized they were getting recruited when colleges were scouting me. A few more people wanted to play for our team.

In my junior year the NCAA allowed one phone call each week, and the letters turned into phone calls. A lot of the college coaches would call my

"I think we knew we had an elite athlete in our family when our mailbox was full of mail from schools interested in Monica. It was during her sophomore year at North Salinas."

Julie Abbott, Monica's mother

coaches, and then my coaches would deliver messages to me. I think they were trying to get a feel for what I wanted and where I wanted to go, but I had no idea. I knew I wanted to go somewhere. Most of the college coaches have a system for recruiting, a process that they go through. But I did not have a process. We were all flying by the seat of our pants. Formal travel leagues have all these systems that they will take you through, but the program I played in didn't have that. So we were all just trying to figure it out. Coach Berg, our travel ball coaches, and our personal coaches contacted college coaches and asked, "Are you interested? What kind of players do you need? Do you have space on the team for this person?" I could ask my coaches, "Why isn't this school recruiting me?" Schools would call me once a week or once a month, but I was so busy that I missed a lot of calls. I had a job. I was playing high school basketball. I played high school softball. I was taking pitching lessons. I missed a lot of calls, and at that time there weren't as many cell phones. I didn't have one.

I was a pretty shy, reserved girl, I guess. I was fairly quiet on the calls, but coaches would talk a lot about their school, and they would always try to get me to talk. "How many brothers and sisters do you have?" They would fire off questions—question after question. Coach Karen Weekly, from the University of Tennessee, made most of the phone calls to me, and it was more like a conversation than firing off questions. I would say the conversation flowed better with her. She would ask me about softball. She would ask me about basketball a lot—like how my team was doing. How were my practices going? She talked to me about school and everyday stuff. She talked about Tennessee—the city, the program, what they were wanting to do with the softball program, their history. I would say the calls usually lasted about thirty minutes—they weren't short. I knew they were in the building stage. It appealed to me because I knew that relationships and people matter.

Lots of things factored into my selection process. Some of the schools simply eliminated themselves, sending letters just to see if I was interested, to see if they could get a response. They didn't put forth much effort—an "I am going to send this to you because you just never know" kind of thing. Meanwhile, others probably got recruits from other schools, so that took them out of the running. I narrowed it down, and soon the time came to start making decisions. The conversations became a little bit tougher.

One of the schools close to where I lived was Stanford—my dad's dream school. My dad's kind of nerdy and smart. I was smart, too—I was eighth in my class and had a 4.3 GPA at one time—but then I took the standardized tests and didn't break the minimum. I was trying to decide if I wanted to go there. Stanford was recruiting me, but my test score wasn't quite high enough. Should I get tutoring? My parents were really pushing me. They were saying, "We will find a way to get you tutoring to help you raise your test scores."

The head coach was super nice and really wanted me to go there. I went on a few visits, and I liked it. I felt like it was a good spot for me. And then the decision was resolved. We were at a tournament, and at this point a school could have one contact with you—if you were at a tournament. The Stanford pitching coach came up to me and said, "How's it going?" And I was interested, but deep down I knew my test scores were not that good. At the same time, I knew I was smart enough to go there. And then she started to talk to me about whether I was interested, asking, "When are you taking your tests?" I started to get more confident. I asked her, "I wanted to ask you about pitching. What kind of style of pitching are you going to teach?" And she said to me, "Right now you are a linear pitcher, and we are going to make you change immediately into being a figure four."

There are two main styles of pitching, and figure four is what I would call a traditional style of pitching. What you watch on TV right now is mostly linear. Almost everyone is linear. There are a few people who throw figure four, but if they do, it is because they were taught by someone that is older. They are completely different styles. It is like comparing a textbook to a

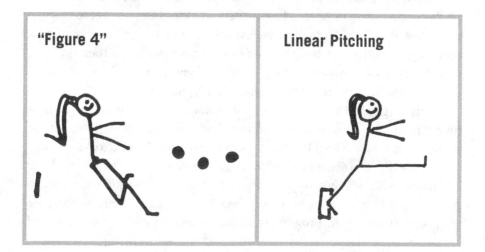

mystery novel. She was saying, "The first thing I am going to do with you—I don't care how good you are—is that I am going to make you a figure four pitcher." I said, "So, you don't like my style of pitching?" I just stood there dumbfounded.

We had already scheduled tutoring. I was going to retake the test. We thought this was a realistic option. I talked with my mom and dad, saying, "I'm sorry, Dad, it's not going to happen. I am not going to be a figure four pitcher. There is no way. I can't do it." My mom would have been happy with any college. She just wanted me to go to college. My dad said, "Aw man, I wanted you to get a Stanford education. It would have been awesome. But you are right; you don't need to be a figure four pitcher."

Softball is such a small world. Never burn a bridge, because things always come full circle. The way you treat people is important. What you say to people is important. Years later, that Stanford coach ended up coaching the USSSA Pride. The Pride was the rival of the Scrap Yard Dawgs, where I played as a pro. It was her first year there. They went 26–0. They were winning everything. Then they played against us, the Scrap Yard Dawgs, in the finals, and we whupped 'em. And every time to this day, when I see her coaching on TV, I always go back to that moment in high school. She's the person behind the hat.

I had a ton of these little meetings at the travel ball tournaments with coaches who came to watch my games. Alabama was there a lot, UCLA, and Florida. At the time, Florida's head coach was Karen Johns. I really wanted to go there. They were in my top five at the time, and they were recruiting me pretty heavily. We had lots of conversations with them. And then suddenly, they stopped recruiting me. They were pretty persistent, and then they just pulled back. I asked my coach, "Can you call them? Just see if they are interested. I'm reading into the signals here. What's going on?"

Coach Berg called and told Coach Johns about my concerns. At our next tournament, Florida was there, and they had a one-on-one with me at the tournament. Coach Karen Johns said—and remember, I was sixteen—"Look, we were really interested in you. We really wanted you to become a Gator and come to Florida, but we just received a transfer from the University of Arizona. She is going to be here next year. We can't have you come. You are too good to come to the program to sit on the bench for two years." She said that to me—a sixteen year old. She just said it straight up to me: "You are too good to come to this program, and we couldn't say 'no' to this pitcher. This pitcher that is coming in is really good. And we need someone immediately. And that's why we were really recruiting you hard. But you are one of the top recruits, and there is no guarantee you will come here. So we are going to pull back on recruiting you, because we picked up a transfer. You should be going to a school where you can start." She was concerned about her program. She was straight up and honest. She had good touch and communication. (Full circle here, ten years later, Coach Karen Johns ended up being a part of the 2008 Olympic Coaching Committee. In 2020, she was on the selection committee to make the team. She has been one of the biggest advocates not only for me but for the sport of softball.)

My top five were Alabama, Florida, Tennessee, UCLA, and Arizona State.

Tennessee was steady in the mix. I was interested in them, but as an up-and-coming program, were they really going to be that good? Also, Tennessee was really far away from home. Alabama was in the mix; I was talking to them pretty regularly. I just didn't have the feeling that it was my place. Which is weird, because now I love their head coach, Pat Murphy. Today we have a good relationship. At the time, I just didn't have that connection.

In addition to coming to the tournaments, college coaches used to do in-home recruiting visits where they would come to your house. I had an in-home visit with Tennessee. My parents had me write a list of questions. We brainstormed in a notebook a list of questions to ask. They knew that I wouldn't ask them if we didn't prepare. My parents said, "This is for you, you've got to ask these questions." My twin sisters, eleven years old at the time, sat with us and took notes. They asked the coaches if I could ever come home if I went to Tennessee. I remember at the end when the coaches asked if I had any more questions, I looked at the sheet, and they had already answered half of the questions. Tennessee came to one of my high school basketball games. That was cool. Tennessee's Coach Weekly told my basketball Coach Darren Jackson that they like to have athletes who have two-sport backgrounds.

I had home visits with UCLA and Arizona State, too. I did unofficial visits to Stanford, Cal Berkley, and UCLA quite a few times. I had official visits scheduled for Alabama and UCLA. I went to Arizona State for an official visit. I had a really good time there. I loved the school and the campus—all of it. The coach, the stadium, all are top notch. At the end of the trip, the coach called me into her office by myself, and I had to sit in her office and talk to her about whether I was going to come. I didn't expect that question to come so directly, and I wanted to avoid saying that I hadn't decided yet. So, when the coach leaned forward and asked, "Are you going to come to Arizona State? Can I count on you to be a Sun Devil?" I was tongue-tied—a seventeen year old, sitting on the other side of the desk, and saying, "I, I, I, uh, uh, uh, I'm not ready yet to decide. I want to see all my choices."

My next official visit was to Tennessee. Both of my parents came, too. My parents and I agreed that if we were asked to decide while we were there, we would not commit until returning home, because this was a big decision. They told me, "We know we like it, but we've got to make sure we are making the right decision. You don't want to just jump in and make a choice." They were also concerned about the travel, so we were not going to make any decision until we were all the way back home. Mom and Dad said, "So, if the coaches try to corner you, then we say no." But hats off to the coaches, because they never once pressured me by asking, "Oh, are you going to come to Tennessee? What is your decision? Who are your top three? Are we in the top running?" They never did anything like that. I think they had asked me once on the phone, "Are we in your top three? Are you interested in us?" That was the most they did. On the visit they never put a lot of pressure on me.

Tennessee was actually playing Florida in football that weekend. It was ESPN Game Day on the day of my recruiting trip, so we were on the field for this game. I remember Coach Karen Weekly saying how much she liked the ESPN analyst, Kirk Herbstreit. We met all of them. I got to take pictures with them. It was a really big deal and very fun. The game was close until the third quarter. Tennessee ending up losing badly. And even though it was pouring rain—I'll never forget it—the stadium just stayed full. No one left. I thought that was so impressive. Fans were still there. Rain was pouring, the team was losing, but we were having the most fun. We were in the student section during the football game. I remember thinking that if fans show up like this for football, imagine how they could show up for softball. Imagine if you could hook them in for softball!

I toured all the facilities. We met the team. We had a lunch with the team, too. Everything turned out well. Co-Head Coaches Ralph and Karen Weekly were there. The pitching coach at the time was Michelle Granger. She had come to one of my high school softball games.

I remember that this place felt like home. I loved that it was on the water. I am from close to the water, so I wanted to be near water. And then when I arrived, everything was future Lady Vol Monica Abbott—jersey, a gift basket in the hotel room, and all that stuff. It was all presented nicely. I got to meet Coach Pat Summitt, who said something like, "Are you sure you don't want to play basketball—or both? If you stay around, come join me for your fifth year." I met football coach Phillip Fulmer. I met Joan Cronan, director of women's athletics.

And I loved that Knoxville in general is not necessarily a big city. It is similar to where I am from. It didn't feel overwhelming or too big. I loved that it was a sports school that prioritized women's sports. I thought it was awesome that they had separate weight rooms for the men's and women's sports teams. I don't think high school athletes understand what that means on a big concept level. I think subconsciously I knew how big of a deal it was. I saw how much pride they took in women's sports, and that meant a lot to me as a female athlete. Not everybody does that. Not everybody has to do that, but I thought, "Here is a school and a community choosing every day to make a choice to support men's and women's sports." Not everyone does that.

We came home from the Tennessee trip and discussed my options. One thing we were concerned about was travel. My mom said, "Basically, the closest school is Stanford, but we're not going there. Monica, it's either a five-hour flight or a six-hour drive." It was almost too practical. I felt like they wanted it to be my decision.

In Salinas I played with Lindsay Schutzler when I was in the twelve and under club team. In school during some of our more epic battles, she transferred to Notre Dame High School. The

> "There were two things going against Tennessee in competing for Monica according to recruiters: 2,500 miles and no softball history at Tennessee. Would the best player in the country come to the last-place team in the SEC?"
>
> Ralph and Karen Weekly, Co-Head Coaches, University of Tennessee

Monica (*right*) and North Salinas High classmate Jennifer Patterson sign papers committing them to college athletic scholarships, November 2003.

rivalry was more about the school than us. She committed to Tennessee. And she was saying, "Monica, why don't you come on to Tennessee? Come on." I was taking my time because I had other options as well. Coaches Ralph and Karen Weekly talked about the program they were building and the pieces they still needed. Because I played against Lindsay, and I played with her, I knew we would be good together on a team. I knew that she was an asset for Tennessee. I knew if she was there, I would have at least one good hitter.

A week later I committed to Tennessee. I called Coaches Ralph and Karen Weekly on a Wednesday and said, "Are you guys both there?" I had them both on the phone. And they closed the office door. I remember walking them into it. I didn't just say, "Okay, I am coming." I made it fun. I think I said something from our conversations. I said, "I want to be the person to change the program. I think I can do it." Then I remember both coaches on the other end of the line just started screaming. Karen said that Ralph ran up and down the hallway.

Then I had to call Coach Pat Murphy at Alabama and Coach Sue Enquist at UCLA to say thank you for recruiting me, but I decided to go to another school. I committed in November right before national letter of intent day for softball. I signed and we had big ceremony at my school.

Everyone was excited, and I could go into my summer and senior year enjoying life. When I made the decision, I think it was a relief for me and for my parents. The recruiting process is not stressful, but it is a lot to deal with. At the time there were a many different rules, regulations, and teams. You want to know where your future is going. And you want to be comfortable with the choice that you made.

When I decided to go to Tennessee, that shocked the softball world. I was one of the top recruits in the country; they expected me to go to UCLA or fall into one of the programs that have always been the top in softball. It changed the forecast of the SEC. I don't think I understood that I had that power. I just felt that I was making the best decision for me when I chose Tennessee. I said, "Women's department—hello, this is awesome! We are going to support women's sports. These fans are sitting out in the rain, and they are staying. Wait until softball comes and gets established!" Look at these softball fans today. They've got these Tennessee crazies showing up all the time. I could see that future, and the community seemed similar to where I am from, and they support their sports the way Salinas does. Coach Ralph Weekly was an Olympic coach, and we thought that was good, offering me an opportunity to create my future in softball if I wanted to. Whereas if I went to some of these other big schools, no matter how good I was, there could be a pecking order. Where would I be able to establish myself?

I remember Coach Sue Enquist at UCLA saying, "You know, Monica, we could win a national championship tomorrow and be on page twenty-six of the *LA Times*." I thought, "What, you are not going to be on the front page?" It was almost like some coaches shot themselves in the foot. They took themselves out of the game instead of staying the course. I remember at one of UCLA's home visits I had to ask, "Now, I have heard that some people only get books, or they only do this; what is the actual scholarship offer you are going to make to me?" They weren't up front about it. I think that ended up hurting them. I thought, "Do they even want me, or am I just another person to them?" Tennessee stayed the course. They stayed the course because they either thought they were a long shot or just kept going because they thought that I might commit. And then it ended up working out. When I did commit there, it rocked the softball world, because everyone was expecting me to go to UCLA.

Looking back on it now, UCLA might have been a little bit nicer because my parents would have been able to come to more games. On the other hand, going to UT gave my twin sisters and my brother more time with my parents. I think my sisters and brother often got a back seat to what I was doing. My schedule was so full. Being farther from home allowed my parents to focus more on the younger ones. Both of my younger sisters got scholarships. Bina played softball for Towson University for four years. Gina played volleyball for one year at a small school. Tenneessee ended up being the good choice for me and my future.

Life Is . . .

Written by R. Bruce Abbott for Monica, his daughter, during her senior year of high school.

★

What advice can a father give his daughter to live by, when she is leaving home on A softball scholarship? It is often thought that parents are the embellishment of Wisdom and guidance.

The truth is we took it one pitch at a time and now it's the bottom of the seventh. We're ahead by one run, but the count's full. There are two outs. And there are Runners at second and third. What do I say at the conference on the mound of life?

The road will be hard, it's supposed to be.
The practice will overshadow life's everyday occurrences.
The time and energy will take respect, dedication, and perseverance.
The work is the foundation that supports your achievement.

There is no love like your family's for they know who you are, not what you are.
Those that helped, shared the values of who you are, not what you are.
Those that will help have the same values of who you are, not what you are.
Those that will use you only know what you are, not who you are.

Friends are loyal.
Friends know your humility.
Friends helped.
Everyone else is just that.
Love will help who you are.
Lovers will take what you are.

Treat life like the gift it is.
Every impression is like a pitch, you don't know how it's received until it's caught.
Every person is like a batter; you know nothing about them until they bat.
Every day is like an inning, you pour yourself into it and know not what you've
    accomplished until it's over.
Every life is like a game, you always know what you have done but never know the
Outcome until you look down from the floors of heaven.

In the end the congratulations will be few and far between.
And your joys will be in watching your prodigy's accomplishments, knowing you
Were blessed with the opportunity to participate in the hardest championship
Game they will ever play, ——— Life.

With all a father's Love,
                Your Dad.

FIVE 2,500 MILES FROM HOME IN BIG ORANGE COUNTRY

I came to Tennessee in the fall after my summer ball season. It was late August in 2003. I came with my mom. We flew out there, and I just brought what I could fit into two big suitcases. I brought a box of pictures of my friends from high school. I never opened the box, but I brought it. We ended up buying a lot of dorm stuff there because I couldn't travel with much on the plane. I remember being really excited. I got all my books, and it was the first time I had a cell phone—Yay! Finally! Cell phones weren't popular when I was in high school. I remember that being a big deal.

I got to meet all the other people there, all my teammates. I remember being overwhelmed because everything was so big, and I constantly got lost. When I came to Tennessee, I was reserved and shy. I was still maturing as far as growing into my own body. I wasn't very confident or comfortable in my own skin. I had friends, but I wasn't very outgoing. My freshman year I was assigned a dorm room with freshman teammate Brittany Bessho. We knew each other. I think it was good because we got along, and Brittany had a car. Our softball field was off campus at the time, so we had to drive there.

I remember worrying about whether I would fit in. On the field I am always fine; it's my bread and butter. I feel comfortable there. But I felt like I didn't fit in as well off the field. Was this what I thought it was going to be? I think other people felt that way toward me, too, my freshman year—which I had a little bit of a hard time with. People, especially in softball, had expectations for me, because obviously Coaches Ralph and Karen Weekly had talked to everyone about me coming in. When someone talks a lot about you coming in, it creates expectations for how you are going to act—what is this person going to be like? Is she really going to change the program? It creates all this chatter, which is cool but also intimidating. I think that was hard for me to deal with. I was in a softball bubble growing up, so my eyes weren't really open to things yet. I hadn't really experienced a lot of life. I wasn't in great shape coming from high school to college. But people had judgements or expectations about me without getting a chance to know me first. There was an expectation around how I was going to be before I could figure out who I was myself. That stung a little bit.

Before my freshman year in college, I had never lifted a weight—never. I had spent most of my time on the softball field practicing. We would do agility drills and biometrics, like running form and footwork. But I hadn't really lifted weights. For two weeks we had training before we started practice to get settled, and, wow, for a week all of us freshmen were just dying. I was so sore it hurt to walk. It was just miserable. Our bodies were wrecked, and we would come home every day, flex, and say, "Look guys, I got a new muscle. Check this out!" Just to be sure it wasn't just me, I would point to a body location and ask, "Do you hurt here too?"

It was hard. It was so hard. One time I will never forget is when we were doing abs to build core. It was like toe touches, right? First off, I didn't have any abs. I was trying to do these toe touches. And the coach said, "Thirty toe touches as a team. If I don't see one of you touch your toes, everyone is going to start over." So, we keep doing them, and I didn't realize it, but I was the one not touching her toes. We kept having to start over, and one of the seniors was yelling, "Who's not touching her toes?" We were supposed to be doing thirty toe touches, and we ended up doing about three hundred. And finally, the coach said, "It's you, Monica." And I was like, "Wha-a-a-at?"

I couldn't reach! My legs were too long, and my core was too weak.

I would say lifting weights was a benefit for me because I had strength and conditioning coaches who knew what they were doing. I think it really helped me because my legs, back, and shoulders got strong. We did a lot of pulling and resistance style or band resistance style on the upper body. It made by arm whippy and strong on the inside. The coaches were good about managing body types. A lot of the girls would do squats, but the coach helped me—a taller player—build up strength in other areas first to be able to squat eventually. I did a lot of leg press and hamstring curls and a LOT of lunges. They had these sandbags over my shoulders, and the conditioning coach knew I was getting stronger, and the coaches told him to push me. All of a sudden, every week, it would be ten more pounds on lunges. I would have this giant sandbag on my shoulders, and he would come over and put another sandbag on my shoulders while I was doing lunges—all the time.

Or we would be doing a manual resistance with a partner, and your partner resists your arm going down. This is a simple exercise without using weights. And that is the one exercise where you feel like you are going to catch a break, because your friend might be easier on you as your partner. But the coach would cut in and say, "Nope, I've got Monica." I was just dying; the coach was so hard on me. I think he knew I could do it; I just didn't know. It helped build up mental strength, confidence, and toughness, and it also proved to myself that I could do it.

Weightlifting helped my pitching, too. I went from throwing sixty-eight mph sometimes to throwing seventy mph! That's a big jump! And each year I was at college, my speed got better. By the time I was a senior, I was pitching seventy mph consistently—and sometimes hitting seventy-three mph. My speed increased, my power increased—all of it. My stamina and muscle endurance really increased, too. It's probably because the coach made me do those lunges.

I was busy in high school, but time management was more difficult in college. We would lift early in the morning at 6:00 a.m. Then I would go to class until noon, have lunch, and then go straight to the softball field until 5:00 p.m. Then I would get treatment, eat dinner, shower, and have to be at study hall. We had to get twelve hours of study hall every week.

I got homesick quite a bit. I called my mom crying a lot. Now as I look back, I think I was more sad and lonely than homesick. I just missed them. Most of my friends my freshman year were all in sports. Mostly I hung out with the softball team and a little bit of basketball, soccer, a couple of track people.

I had a little bit of a culture shock—the distance from home, and the weather was mind-blowing to me. I had never experienced four seasons. So I went to Tennessee, and I know it is a moderate climate in the southern states. Yet I would go outside, and it would be nice, and I would just be sweating from the humidity. And then weather forecasted a light rain, and it would be torrential—soaking you. I can't tell you how many times I got just soaked walking to class, because I had no idea it was going to pour like that. It would be fifty degrees and that was okay, seemed kind of normal, but it would begin snowing. I couldn't figure this weather out. What was I supposed to wear? I remember in high school I wore sandals to school a lot. So that is what I brought to college. I wore a sweatshirt a lot. I didn't really have a big jacket or anything.

So, I called home frequently, mainly because of the stress of the schedule or the stress of softball. Not only was I sore twenty-four seven from working out, but I was also starting to do school—and for the first time in my life, I was not doing well in school. Not because of lack of effort; I struggled in those huge classes in the big lecture halls, psychology 101 and geology 101. So, I was having a hard time with those classes; I was struggling in school. I was getting my ass kicked every day in the weight room—and running. And then I had a team that had these expectations of me or pre-judgments of who I was as a person without getting to know me first.

And then I had Coaches Ralph and Karen Weekly, who told me a story when I was being recruited, and now when reality hit, I was struggling. Had they been telling me the truth? This isn't what they said Tennessee would be like. When they recruited me, they told me that their pitching coach, Michele Granger, who lived close to my home area in California, came to UT once a month. I was especially excited to learn from her, a softball legend who led the US Olympic Team to the gold in 1996—the team that first inspired me as a little girl to be an Olympian. I did not see Michele Granger at all my freshman year until a pre-season tournament. I saw her only one time after that. This caused a little bit of tension with Karen and me, because Karen was taking over some of the pitching. I needed a pitching coach. I knew what a good pitch felt like; I knew what it was supposed to look like. But I couldn't put it into words yet. I didn't know how to describe what I was feeling. If you can't put it into words, it can be more difficult to communicate with a coach to get better. You've got to be able to describe it. In high school you are just doing it—pitching. In college you are refining it, speaking about it.

They had someone they recruited for third base catching me. She was struggling to catch the ball, and then a senior, Lauren Mattox, who would help in the bullpen, suddenly became a starting catcher because she could hit. And she was struggling as well. I didn't really have a solid catcher behind home plate. So that was a problem my freshman year, too.

They were trying to get me to perform better for them, doing anything they could to help me improve. So that was very stressful, and on top of that, I was homesick. I wanted to see my parents, my family—see how my sister was doing. And I would call my mom, and I would be upset, and she would say, "Monica, you wanted to do this." About halfway through the semester, my parents started giving me tough love. They said, "Look, this is a good decision for you. Just stick it out. Keep going." I remember my mom saying, "You're not missing anything here. You are doing what you are supposed to be doing. You are not missing anything here. I still go to work every day. And when you come home, I will still be going to work every day. Everything will be right here when you come back."

There were other differences, too. The way a softball field is built in the south is completely different from the west coast because of the weather. They mostly use the Georgia clay in the SEC. It is like red dirt. But in California, it is usually like a light brown dirt or grey dirt—really thin and powdery and super hard. At Tennessee, it is sticky. Your cleats stick in it. Just weird things you didn't think about; I wouldn't have thought the field would feel different.

The surface levels of stadiums are different, too, which can be a factor for a player. The grounds in some stadiums are harder than others—some are softer. There are definitely ways that people use the dirt to help them. The University of Georgia infield is so hard it feels like cement. It eats up infielders. At Tennessee, when I was there, our main offense consisted of slappers* Sarah Fekete, India Chiles, and Lindsay Schutzler, and then we had four or five good power hitters. But for those three slappers, Ralph would say, "If we can get them on, then we will be doing great." So he would pack the dirt, and they would make it as hard as cement. And it would be easier for them to get hits. It sped up the ball through the infield and made bounces higher. But then on the pitching mound, the dirt was so hard that instead of sinking in the way they were supposed to do, my spikes just sat on top, like walking on concrete.

Also impactful is what is behind home plate, what you are looking at. It could feel really close, like the fans are right on you. It can feel spread out. The dimensions can feel very different. The University of Alabama stadium is 190 feet all the way around their outfield—which is a really small field. Someone check swings, and it is a home run. Each field has a different feel, and that makes it fun. At the end of the day though, the mound is still forty-

---

*A slapper is a left-handed hitter who takes advantage of their speed by placing the ball in a spot that gives them the best chance to get on base.

three feet from home plate. The batter's boxes are still the same. You are still outside. You still have to deal with elements. Weather plays a bigger part than people realize.

My freshman year we had our first tournament in Hawaii. This was a really big deal. Everyone was excited. We were all playing well. It was the greatest trip ever! No one had been to Hawaii. This was so cool, right? And we were practicing and playing some games there for preseason camp. I think we were playing the University of Hawaii. It was the championship game. There was a hitter up, and I think we were winning 1–0. Karen was calling pitches. So, she called a pitch. And I shook her off, "No." Karen gave the call to the catcher again, and I said, "No." At this point there were not a lot of people in the stands. (I got in so much trouble for this, by the way.) She called the pitch again and yelled, "Throw the pitch!" I looked at her and I was like—"No." I threw the pitch I wanted to throw—the one I felt most comfortable and confident with. The girl struck out. And then Karen was furious with me. She said, "You throw the pitches I call." And I yelled back at her. This was in the dugout. She escalated to level twenty. Our teams were watching. Everyone was watching. This was in the middle of the third inning.

She yelled at me, "You throw the pitches I call. I am the coach. I did the research. You throw the pitches I call." I looked back at her, and I probably matched her level of intensity saying, "I am not going to throw a pitch I am not comfortable throwing. That's the last thing you should do. If I don't feel comfortable throwing it, I am not going to throw it. That's why I shook you off. And we got her out!" Honestly, I probably had too much sass for the moment. I was shaking, and I couldn't believe I was saying that. This was my freshman year—my first tournament! So, the game continued. We went on to win the game. I didn't say anything to anybody. Everyone on the team was mad at me. I was in the doghouse.

Ralph and Karen called me into their meeting room later that night. They sat me down and said, "Monica, we just had a meeting with some of the seniors and upperclassmen, and they are upset that you did this—that you didn't respond to them. They are also mad at us, because they don't feel like we punished you the right way." I should have been pulled from the game is what they basically said. I should have been pulled from the game. But I stayed in because I was the number-one pitcher. The team didn't think that was fair or right. At this point, I was not mad. I was just listening. I was in the principal's office—scared. I had never been in trouble in my life, and now I had yelled at my coaches, and this "angel" was in trouble. Ralph and Karen both looked at me and said, "It is not working, you and Karen in the bull pen and all this stuff. It's just not working. There are too many arguments. It is too stressful." I said, "Stop trying to change me or make me into something I am not. I would rather go down losing on a pitch that I was committed to than throwing a pitch and not be committed and lose." They went on, "We are just butting heads. Things are not going right." I said, "I know. I agree. Things aren't working out. Maybe this isn't the right place for me. Michele Granger is not here ever. I am sorry for the outburst like that. But I am not going to throw a pitch I am not comfortable with. I don't think that is right to do. You have to be committed to what you are doing, otherwise you are going to lose. The outcome is not going to be what you want." They said a lot of stuff to me about having a bad attitude—being a bad teammate and being a bad athlete. They said, "Maybe we don't want you." They threatened to kick me off the team—to pull my scholarship.

The next day they said, "We are going to throw live (inter-squad scrimmage) and you are going to pitch."

"Okay," I said.

They said, "Every time someone touches the ball, you are going to have to run a foul pole—down and back of the outfield line—after you are done pitching. Now I had to serve the sentence for the crime. I thought I was just doing the right thing for the team. But the team persecuted me. Mind you, if you know my pitching style, you know I throw hard. I had to face twenty hitters. People fouled a lot in general. And they counted every foul ball. I had to run thirty-two or thirty-six foul poles. I had to run all these foul poles and do pitching speed drills, and I think my teammates started to feel sorry for me a little bit. They finished practice an hour and a half later, and I was still out there for what felt like forever. I don't really remember much after that. It hurt my confidence a little bit. It definitely hurt my heart. It made me question, "What am I doing? Do I want to be here? Is this the right place for me?" It made me question whether I was a good pitcher. Should I be shaking off pitches? I didn't even know it was a controversial thing to shake off a pitch. It shut me down. I was like a wounded dog. It made me put my tail between my legs. Even when I wanted to speak up about something that I didn't agree with, I remained silent. It shut me down.

The coaches said, "When we go back to practice, in Tennessee, we are going to come up with something." We resolved our issues, saying, "Let's just keep going forward and try to communicate better." It comes down to communication. Karen and I had a breakdown in communication—and also probably a breakdown in expectations that were not clear-cut from the beginning. I expected that I could shake a pitch. That was always accepted in my career with any of my coaches I played for. It was not something we had talked about, and I got punished for it.

In the end I think I was wrong. I should not have yelled across the field at Karen, especially in the middle of a game. I can take full blame for that. In the heat of the moment in competition you don't think about those things—you just react. I was young and there was already tension in that relationship. That was the blow-up moment. Both of us had our adrenaline running—our competitive fire going. Both of us wanted to win. The problem was that we both thought we wanted to win more than the other one. One of us wanted to win. One of us wanted control. That's what it boiled down to. My coaches had not developed a personal relationship with me. I needed compassion and care. When you don't set expectations or communicate expectations early, then it is hard to go after what you want or what the team needs in the heat of the moment, because you get fired up.

Breakdown of communication . . . breakdown of expectations . . . safe space to communicate. . . that's one word that is thrown around a lot these days. People are not going to communicate well if they are not comfortable. And that was me—I wasn't comfortable. I wasn't comfortable with Karen in the bullpen. Looking back on that now, it sounds so senseless. Why did that happen the way that it happened? I think it was because of the breakdown in communication prior to that game in Hawaii—just the overall tension in the relationship—someone being in the bullpen that maybe didn't necessarily know how to teach pitching. She was just trying to execute workouts for me, and I did not understand that.

Have you ever met a kid who is eight years old but looks like she is eighteen? That was me. I feel like they had that feeling toward me—expecting more from me. And then on top of that, I was an exceptional athlete. I was a big kid in an adult body. I towered over everyone. Karen and I really bumped heads, because I knew what I was supposed to do; I knew what it was supposed to feel like; I knew what throwing a curveball looked like, but

I couldn't put any of it into words. I also knew what she was telling me to do wasn't necessarily what I was taught to do. I thought, "Oh, should I trust you to do this? You told me I was going to have a pitching coach, and they are not here." There was a breakdown of trust. That tournament in Hawaii was an accumulation of everything in one moment.

After that, they basically told me that they were thinking about just sitting me. They threatened me. They said, "You don't need to go to Tennessee, we don't need you here. We are thinking about pulling your scholarship because you can't get along." They called me a problem child. "If you are not going to do it our way, you can leave," they said.

Karen had recruited me. I had a lot of long conversations with her on the phone. So, in person, the fact that we didn't get along was weird. I thought we were going to get along great. I know now that the bullpen probably wasn't where she was comfortable. It was rocky from there on out—until I was a late junior or senior. I got along with Ralph fine. He would joke around with me. He was personable in the way he taught me. It was like that a lot. The team at the time was saying, "The coach would not have stood for that with someone else, but you still got to pitch." In my head, I was thinking like any athlete, that I was not going to do something I was not comfortable with. That continued to happen going into my freshman season. There were quite a few issues—arguments and things like that.

They used to ask me, "How do you want to be coached? How do you want to be talked to?" And I would say, "I want to be coached. I want you to tell me what I am doing wrong or what I can do better." I would always say that I liked to be challenged, but I meant that I liked to be challenged in a positive way. When I said I wanted to be challenged, they took it as yelling, like Ralph yelling, "Don't walk the first batter of the inning. No free bases. How many home runs are you going to give up?" Yelling and getting in my face—they did it that way. When I was saying I wanted to be challenged, I was thinking about Coach Keith saying, "Okay, Monica, let's do location practice on your rise ball. You got five for five, are you going to be able to get six for six? Okay, you've got six, are you going to miss seven? I don't think you can get ten." That's the kind of fun, playful banter I was used to. And there was intention with it. I was challenged. And then I went to an atmosphere that was in your face. And I struggled adjusting to that. It made me put my head down and my tail between my legs and not say much.

In softball, shaking off a pitch is controversial. I had always been taught that you never throw a pitch that you're not 100 percent committed to. Usually, you are on the same page as the coach, and things really flow. This is my philosophy in general for shaking off a pitch: you don't shake off a pitch because you want to throw something else. But there are times when you know it is not a good pitch, and you know the one that should be thrown instead. You just intuitively, instinctively know as an athlete, as a pitcher, based on what your pitches look like that day—what the umpire zone is, what the hitter looks like, or the hitters' previous at-bats, and the catcher knows a lot of times, too. You just instinctively know.

Playing in the Southeastern Conference gave me new challenging experiences. We were playing Alabama at their home stadium. I was doing really well in SEC play. I kept striking all these people out because that is what I do, right? They couldn't hit off of me. So, their right-handed hitters—they decided their feet should not just touch the line in the batter's box but fully go over the line. I swear I probably hit thirty people in the game. They were leaning all over the strike zone—over home plate. That was their strategy— get hit. Stand on top of the plate. Monica will either hit you or walk you because I was throwing the pitch outside a lot. That's how they tried to hit off of me.

I have the record for most strikeouts, but I probably also have the record for most hit batters because of that game. Standing at the plate, they would turn to their side a little over the plate to get hit by the ball in the quad. That was their strategy. And it was awful. It was not cheating because they were within the rules. But it was a gray area, and they knew it. In the SEC, stuff like that happened to me all the time. Georgia did it a lot, as did Auburn. At the time it sucked that people did stuff like that to me. But holy cow, it made me so good, because now if people try to do it, or at the Olympics try to do it, I just laugh and say, "Go ahead, stand there. I've been there before." It challenged me and made me better.

People would say, why do you keep hitting batters? And I responded, "They are trying to get hit themselves. Why aren't they standing in the box? The ball is over the plate. That is a strike technically. They are literally getting hit by pitches that are strikes." Now that rule has changed. Hitters must attempt to make a move (out of the way) if the pitch is judged a strike by the umpire.

Getting ready to whip the ball in there for the Lady Vols during the Women's College World Series. The pitching circle is hardly big enough to hold the four-time UT All-American. Courtesy of the University of Tennessee Athletics Department.

I don't remember how it ended up happening, but my freshman year we won the Eastern Division, and we lost in regionals. I don't know why we did it the way we did it, but this team was winning and there was this big weather delay. And I was super sick. I was coming down with the flu, and they still had me pitch. We ended up losing. The game had started at 11:45 p.m., but we did not leave the field until 3:00 a.m. I don't know why they allowed that game to happen. They should have rescheduled it or delayed it.

My freshman year I stayed for summer school mini term to get credits and to train. I was thinking I might as well get extra credits while I could. I didn't know what would happen if I had to sit out or lose my scholarship. And it would give me a chance to decide what I wanted to do. I was talking to Keith and Kenny. And I was talking to a couple of friends of mine who went to other schools to see if there was space for me. And then I went home after the mini term.

I had talked to my coach about what happened in Hawaii, and my parents knew about it. I told coaches Berg and Gardner. They knew how good I was and what was going wrong. They also knew what kind of person I am. My parents were wondering what was going on with me. Is Monica going wild in her freshman year of college just partying all the time and they hate her? She never had an attitude, and she sometimes doesn't speak up enough. They were concerned and they started to come out once a month or every other month to see what was actually happening. They became worried about my general well-being.

I was always really close with Keith, because I spent a lot of time with him at the softball field. And I think I ended up telling him more than anyone. I asked him to see if there was another school that was interested in me. I didn't want to transfer, but I wondered, "Do I need to?"

And so I started to look at a couple of schools. Maybe this was something I needed to do—go back close to home. I had not put out any feelers. I had conversations with my coaches at home and my parents. Should I transfer or do I want to stick it out one more year? What should I do here? What is best for me?

Apparently, the word started getting around. In July I was watching and supporting one of my sisters playing at a softball tournament, and Ralph and Karen showed up. Karen asked me to go to lunch with her and someone else. At lunch she said, "Look, we heard that you are thinking of transferring, and

we don't want you to go anywhere. We know that last year was tough." This
was a really big deal for me, because I didn't speak up a lot about things I
wanted or things I thought because I wasn't allowed to anymore. I remember saying, "I need a pitching coach." The lunch went on, and I said, "Look,
we don't have a pitching coach, and you and I in the bullpen isn't working. I
need a coach that is there to help me. Just because I can't say what I'm doing
doesn't mean that I don't know what I am doing. Teach me how to talk about
pitching. I don't know how to put it into words." I said it plain and simple
like that.

A little time passed at lunch, and then she said, "We have been talking
about it as well. There is someone that we know that we are trying to get
to be our pitching coach." And that's how I learned about Marty McDaniel.
They said he was a men's fastpitch pitcher. His dad played.

Tennessee ended up letting Michele Granger go to get someone full time.
They hired Marty McDaniel in July going into my sophomore year. Things
improved significantly because he took over all the practices for pitchers, and
we also acquired another pitcher, Megan Rhodes. That next year, everything
changed. I don't know if it was maturity or stubbornness and loyalty, but I
thought, "I made this decision; I have a good thing here. We just had a rough
go about it. It didn't run as smoothly as it should have." I knew it was going to
take time to build it. I needed to give them a chance to do it.

It took a while to get adjusted. Once I adjusted, every year got better.
Looking back at it now, I wish I had adjusted a lot faster, but that's growing
up. Part of that is just growth and maturity—all of those things. Not everyone is this way, but I was a late bloomer, physically, socially, and mentally. I
was still coming into that piece when I was a freshman in college.

I think my freshman year was by far the hardest. But that was the year I
learned how to talk about pitching. I was mentally broken down and had to
figure out how to be mentally tough. Do I agree with the way the coaches
challenged me? No. But did it make me a better player? Absolutely.

When my sophomore year of college rolled around in 2005, everyone was super motivated to make the World Series. We had a good freshman class. We had a good sophomore class. That is when Shannon Doepking came in to catch. We had a pitching coach who was very personable and built relationships with people, and that really helped me. Marty was very jovial—very funny—and I still remember some of the first things he told me: "I have been watching you pitch, and I think you can do this, this, and this well. We will try to improve this. I love how you have this little routine. This is important. Make sure you do that when things are going well and when things are going poorly." He was a very relationship-oriented guy and communicated very well. I think part of that was because he understood the pitching position more.

Marty was a great advocate for me. He is probably the reason I stayed at Tennessee. I learned that he had been hired in August after my freshman year. I thought, "At least they are making an effort. Let me give it a chance. Let me make an effort to see how this goes. And then I will decide. It's a lot better already, so let me just give it a chance." Just having the pitching coach—having Marty come in—was night and day for me. There was consistency in the bullpen—a common voice. Stephanie Humphrey, a Lady Vol softball player between 2000 and 2003, became our volunteer assistant. She is four years older than I am. She had a really good changeup and was super bubbly, and she and I got along well, which helped. Meanwhile, Shannon Doepking was a catcher who could handle my speed and movement. That was a big deal, and we got along well, too. They also brought in another pitcher, Megan Rhodes.

So, we had another pitcher that was good. Things got better. Some of this is just part of the building process: you have to find the right pieces.

On the academic side of things, I still had yet to declare a major. I went to college wanting to be a high school athletics director or a physical therapist. My freshman year, I was really reserved, very nervous, and shy. Put me on the softball field, and I was an extrovert saying, "Come on, let's go." In life off the field, I was an introvert. All freshmen had to take a speech 101 class. We had to give so many speeches, and I was struggling so much. Shaking, I would be speaking, holding a sheet of paper, or working with the podium,

> "It's fun to coach someone who is a top one-percenter—and she was a one-percenter. She was the best pitcher in the world. You don't mess that up."
>
> Marty McDaniel, pitching coach, University of Tennessee

saying, "That was it. Thank you very much." I ended up passing the class and putting it behind me.

In college I always had a little bit of nerves. I was a nervous kind of pitcher, so to speak. When I get nervous, the ball breaks more! It speeds up and then breaks like crazy. I make the pitches too good to swing at, but they are not in the zone. Everything magnifies in a very cool way, but not when a hitter is up—because they are balls. Karen Weekly was really good about helping me with this. She would always talk to me about being nervous—how to channel the nervous energy. Karen would talk with me about breathing, having a routine, what to do when I felt nervous on the mound, and what to do between innings. She would always say it is good to be nervous and to have butterflies. It means you care. She would say, "If you have butterflies, don't let them just fly around like crazy; try to have them fly in formation." Butterflies fly in formation. They clump together and fly together. Even to this day that works for me.

Into my sophomore year, I started to get more comfortable. I was starting to feel more confident in myself and in my surroundings. College advisors wanted me to major in psychology, but I didn't want to major in that. They were trying to shovel student-athletes into majors so that they could graduate. Then a friend of mine on the team, Kat Card, and I were talking about it, and she suggested that I try her major, communication studies. My speech class fears came back to me, and I didn't know if I could do that. We were talking about it, and she said, "Just try a class or two. It is actually a lot more than just speeches. You do public speaking, but it is also about personalities—how to communicate with people. It includes TV or marketing and public relations if you want to be a sports agent or on TV. You should try it." I did and really liked it. I found out that Peyton Manning was a comm studies major! A couple of soccer players that I was friends with were, too. I took a class and thought, "This could be useful for me." I wasn't so great at giving speeches yet, but I was improving—especially when talking about softball. I was trying to get better at speaking. I knew this would be really good for me.

I officially entered the communications department after my sophomore year. That was a great choice for me. The classrooms were smaller. I got to know the teachers in the department. I started to get involved on campus, too. I was on the Student Athlete Advisory Committee (SAAC), a community leadership program. And we organized the first-ever Volscars Event, a program that showcased student-athletes for their accomplishments and their impact on the community. By the time I left after my senior year, I thought I would love to be a motivational speaker or work in marketing, work in team communication or interpersonal communication with groups where you would go into businesses and teach them how to communicate with each other at different levels. By the time I graduated, I absolutely loved it. I thought it would be a useful degree, and it turned out to be ten times its worth. I can write a speech now. I know how to engage with an audience. I know how to use the podium versus a stand-alone microphone. I have a little bit of marketing and a little bit of public relations. It was a good choice for me.

In January 2005 I tried out for the USA National Team and dominated. I literally struck out everyone and made the team. I have always been number 7. I was number 7 as a kid and all through college. I chose this number because we call it the number of completion—seven innings in a game, seven days in a week. God built the world in seven days. One of the Olympians, Amanda Freed, was also number 7, so I had to change my number. We just doubled it, and I became number 14. I feel like now, number 14 has epitomized my professional career. In 2022, I celebrated my fourteenth year in Japan.

After USA National Team tryouts, I went straight to softball season with Tennessee. In my sophomore year when I was up at bat, other SEC team pitchers would deliberately try to hit me. This became a common occurrence. My coaches and I decided that I would only pitch and no longer bat. The risk of getting hurt was too great. I was okay as a batter, but my strength was in pitching. I was happy to step aside and let other more talented hitters shine. This gave me full focus on improving my pitching.

One day I was told that I had a meeting in the basketball arena and had better get over there. "Don't be late; it's Pat Summitt." There I found Candace Parker and Pat Summitt. We had about three or four meetings together—Pat Summitt, Candace Parker, and me. She took the time to invite me. I wasn't on her team. She could have had those meeting just with Candace. She had no reason to include me. Candace and I were both unique athletes on campus at the time. And we are both women, and that part made it cool for me.

We did some leadership development with Pat. It was a late lunch meeting. That is the year Pat started coming out to our softball program—maybe because she liked me. I don't know. I think she just wanted to know me better and know my personality. I asked her, "Will you come talk to my team? It is

"Are you sure you don't want to play basketball?" asked UT Lady Vols basketball coach Pat Summitt on Monica's campus recruiting visit, fall 2002.

cool that I get to do this with you, but would you mind just coming to our team to speak a little bit? We really think we can make the World Series this year. We are all motivated."

And so Pat came out. And that is how we started the tradition of holding our gloves up together at the top of the circle and then down. And that's how we started touching feet during the national anthem. That's when she started talking about the power of a team and the power of trust and touch of each other to be connected. Having that little connection before a game is important for how you play during the game. She ended up throwing the first pitch at one of our home games. Our team did really well. We were excited because we were in the top ten of the rankings. She was following us. I would see her in the lunch hall, and she would say, "Oh, you did great—twelve strikeouts!" Pat really ended up motivating our team a lot.

All of UT's staff did it, too. I saw football coach Phillip Fulmer a lot, and he would talk to me about the games. And J J Clark, track and field coach, loved softball. As softball started to get good, everyone became more invested in it. It was really cool.

Shannon Doepking said maybe we could try to get Pat Summitt to come to the World Series. Shannon, Megan Rhodes, Natalie Brock, India Chiles, Kat Card, Sarah Fekete, and I became really close. We thought, we have got to ask Pat for something. We've got to put her on the spot—Pat Summitt, the basketball coach, the Hall of Famer. We should see if she would come to the World Series! Of course, I had to be the one to ask. So, I said, "Coach Summitt, we want to ask you something as a team. If we make the World Series, it'll be the first time for Tennessee. Will you just come for a game? That would be so cool. You have been such a big influence for us. If we make the World Series, will you come?" And she didn't blink and said, "Yeah, I will come." I said, "Okay, we have to shake on it." And we shook on it. And when we shook, she looked me right in the eye with those eyes, and she said, "Now that's only the World Series in Oklahoma."

We got through regionals and were headed to play super regionals at Stanford, which was awesome because it is the closest school to my house. The entire city of Salinas came out to Stanford, including my high school softball team. I was on the front page of the newspaper in Salinas again. My athletics director and all these people drove up for the game that day.

We ended up beating Stanford in two games! We were on the bus celebrating. And I think it was Natalie Brock or Sarah Fekete or someone in our group who said, "Oh my gosh, you guys, we've got to call Coach Summitt!" The bus was going wild. We were chanting to call Coach Summitt! She was going to come to the World Series. And oh shoot, who is going to call and tell her? At that point Karen came over to calm us down.

Karen handed her phone to me and said, "You can use my phone. You have got to tell her we are going." And so, we put her on speaker, and I was bouncing off the walls at the time. I said, "Hey, Coach Summitt. It is Monica Abbott, the softball player. You remember me, right? I have some good news to tell you. It looks like you're going to the World Series! We won at super regionals! We beat Stanford! It was 2–0. We are going to the World Series next week! You said you would come. So, you will come, right? You are on speaker phone; the whole team is here." She said, "You did? All right, I'll be there. I made a promise to you. We shook on it. I'll be there."

When we first made it, we were bouncing off the walls. We went to dinner to celebrate that we made it, and our families got to come. I remember going back to the hotel and we all jumped into the pool in our jerseys. "We made the World Series for the first time ever!"

But then it became, "Oh, shoot, we made the World Series." We were back to Knoxville, and the turnaround time was really fast. Super regionals ended, then we practiced for two days—and then Tennessee chartered a flight for us! It was the first time ever Tennessee softball got a chartered plane because one of the boosters gave us a plane to go to Oklahoma City. We thought we were the hottest thing ever. And we were!

We went to the World Series, and Pat Summitt came. She was hanging out in the bullpen with the catcher and me. We were taking pictures. She went into the stands. And we were saying, "Wow, look! There is Pat Summitt here to cheer for us." Nowadays, you watch the College World Series, and every main college coach is there from participating universities. Pat Summitt was the first big-time coach to show up at the World Series. How cool is that? I am going to go ahead and claim we made it a thing!

That year we were kind of the Cinderella story—beating the number one seed, Arizona, in the first game. That was phenomenal. I think everyone was nervous, but it was an excited nervous. We couldn't stop talking about how nervous we were. "But I'm excited, but I'm nervous. I'm excited. I'm nervous." The stadium was really nice—one of the nicest we had played in. I remember there was a plexiglass panel with a camera behind it that captured a home plate view. I missed a sign and broke that plexiglass window—oh, the memories! We practiced for a lot of defense and offense, and there were people who really stepped up and did well, like Natalie Brock. She came in and pinch-hit. Tonya Callahan, Sarah Fekete, and Kat Card played well, too. It all happened really fast. It was a celebration and fun. We went to all these famous spots in Oklahoma City. We saw the Oklahoma City bombing site. We went to Bricktown. Everything was exciting and fun and new. We were all just having the time of our lives. That's how it was the first time.

That first year we definitely outperformed other teams. I don't think anyone expected us to do as well as we did. I remember Smokey the mascot came. And I remember we kept saying, "The cheerleaders are here." We had already known the cheerleaders because they were on the Student Athlete Advisory Committee with us. It was a lot of fun. I do remember we had pretty good fan support that showed up at the series. We should have made it to the finals. We beat Michigan but then we lost to them in the elimination game. I just ran out of gas. They pitched me a lot. We knew we could beat them. We knew we were talented enough. After the game, people were coming over and said, "We can't believe we aren't going to the World Series finals.

You pitched phenomenally. That was incredible!" We lost in the final innings. The intensity at the end was something. We ended up coming in third. We had a party at the end when we came back to Knoxville and a little ceremony the next day where all the fans came out. We watched a couple of highlights, there was a speech or two, and we signed autographs.

After my sophomore year, I started traveling with the USA National Team. It was a busy schedule. I don't even think I went home. That was my first year with them. I was so shy and quiet. I just didn't say anything. And I also didn't really play much. I remember we went back to Oklahoma City for a World Cup event. We got to play on that same World Series field. We didn't play very well that year. That was the summer of 2005, and the USA girls were still high off of the Olympic Gold Medal from 2004. I was definitely low on the totem pole. I was more like a cheerer and on the team to see if I would be good. There were three or four other players like that, too.

I remember Jennie Finch that year. She was so sweet. She was kind of like a big sister to me. She had a way of lifting you up. She was very nice about everything, and she, Jessica Mendoza, Stacey Nuveman, and Natasha Watley were all so welcoming to me. Jennie was cool because she would say, "Yeah, you've got to get it together, because you are the next one." She loved that I threw hard. We did play three or four events, but I didn't play a lot. I was the youngest and probably not as mature as everyone else, plus I needed to be tested. You have to try out each year to be on the national team.

I went back to college that fall for my junior year, and I was so motivated. We could make the World Series. This was the year I was really good, but I struggled a little bit as a pitcher. Most people struggle their sophomore year, but I struggled my junior year. I think it was a combination of things. People knew me more from the national team and would get hyped up to play me. I had a boyfriend my junior year, and it probably wasn't a good match. I was

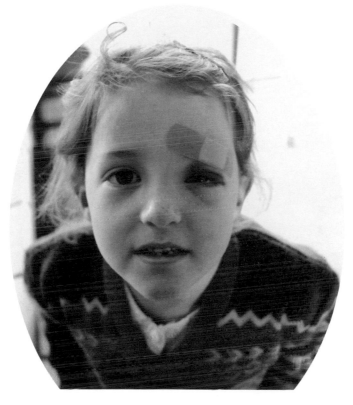

Monica shows off her first softball injury, a black eye and stitches after getting too close to older siblings and cousins practicing with bats.

Monica showed promise at a young age. Here in one of her first big travel ball
tournaments in Illinois, pitching for the Storm.

Looking for a sign from the catcher during a Lady Vols game. This became
Monica's signature pose throughout her career.

Monica and Shannon Doepking embrace after a National Pro Fastpitch championship game win over the USSSA Pride in 2011. Courtesy of Dina Kwit.

Ready for Olympic action with Team USA. Monica had the good fortune to work with many companies including Wilson Softball.

Monica pitches for Team USA in the 2021 Olympic Games. Because of the Covid-19 pandemic, fans were not allowed in the stadium.

Known to be a dedicated trainer with a "practice hard" mentality, Monica demonstrates the trait in this workout—making space and time to develop herself.

Monica and Kazuki Watanabe discuss pitch-calling strategy in a midgame meeting. It is easy to see the large crowd in the background supporting the Toyota team.

The president of the Toyota Motor Company was supportive of the company softball team— so supportive he bought a company bus for the team's away games.

A team "selfie" with Akio Toyoda, the president of Toyota Motor Corporation and a big fan of the Red Terriers softball team.

With UT teammates Lindsey Schutzler (*left*) and India Chiles (*right*). Coach Karen Weekly loved the symbolism of the two leading hitters carried on Monica's shoulders. Courtesy of the University of Tennessee Athletics Department.

distracted—probably not as rested and ready to go as I normally was. For me personally it was more of a down year.

Today I would tell a student-athlete having trouble not to press. I started to press and force it, and that messed me up mentally. I wanted success to happen so badly that I tried to force it instead of focusing on what I did well and allowing things to develop naturally. I thought it couldn't get any worse. I felt like I was letting my team down. I slowly worked my way out of it, but it probably took longer than it should have.

Our team was really good that year. We played Michigan in super region-als to go to the World Series. It was a best of three series. The series was split 1–1. And I will never forget—it was the seventh inning. We were up by one run with one out. They had a runner on first base. Ralph called timeout. He

Monica (*far left* with eyeblack) shows her spirit in a pregame cheer, with UT Lady Vols at the school's first Women's College World Series, 2004. Courtesy of the University of Tennessee Athletics Department.

came out to the mound and said, "I want you to intentionally walk the next two hitters."

I will never forget it. He loaded the bases. He said, "Don't argue with me, because this is what we are doing. I know I always say no walks, but we are going to put these people on base, and then you are going to strike the next two out. And that's how we are going to win this game." He was trying to match up a lefty pitcher with lefty batters—lefty on lefty matchups.

So, at the bottom of the seventh, bases loaded, we were battling the defending national champion Michigan at Tyson Park in Knoxville to get to the World Series, and we were going to strike the next two people out. He gave me a plan and that's what I did. I struck out the next two hitters and we went back to the World Series! It was exciting. We placed third again.

After the college season I played on the national team again at world championships that year. One time I brought the wrong jersey—our red jersey and our blue jersey looked really similar, and I actually brought the wrong color. OMG! And I was supposed to start the game. I did all these dumb things, and it all worked out. We had world championships in China that year—2006. I actually pitched very well there. I think making the team again helped give me confidence. I got to pitch a lot more. They gave me trust and a little more responsibility. I got in really good shape, too. When I came back to Tennessee, people were saying, "Oh, Monica, you are skinny."

Of all the places our national team played, I liked playing in the Oklahoma City Stadium the best. They had the World Cup there. But I liked the stadium in China, too. I thought that was a really cool spot. It was the same stadium for the 2008 Olympic Games, and I pitched great at both of those.

In those years I had good coaches on the national team, Mike Candrea and Chuck D'Arcy. Coach D'Arcy was a men's fastpitch pitcher in his career, and I really liked him. The summer after my junior year, he said, "You need to work on your drop ball more or a change of speed. You need to have one or the other. Right now, your rise ball is so good, your curveball is good, all of that, but you are playing international, and you want to make the Olympic team. You don't need this pitch"—referring to my screwball—"you need something else lower in the zone. You're really good, but you could be so much better. You need to think about throwing fewer side-to-side pitches and more up and down." At that time, I was still throwing a screwball and a curveball. He was right—I didn't have a great drop ball or change.

I came back to Tennessee in the fall. It was my senior year. We had won the world championships in China. I was having a great time. I became close friends with Jessica Mendoza, Stacy Nuveman, Jennie Finch, and Natashia Watley. Vicky Galindo was my roommate. I was finally starting to fit in on the team, and it gave me more confidence going into my senior year.

What Chuck had said stayed in my mind. One day at fall practice, I thought, "I'm not going to throw a screwball anymore. I've got to go cold turkey." Karen was calling screwballs in the scrimmage, but I knew I couldn't throw that anymore. It was a bad idea. So when Karen called the screwball, I told myself, "I am not throwing that. I need to just cut it off." So I started to shake it off. This is what I felt I needed to do. I was on the mound, and she was in the dugout. But the tone of conversation was completely different from my freshman year. After I shook her off about a million times, Karen came to the mound and

"She was mowing people down with 70–72 mph fastball. Like a fool on my radio show, I said, 'I could hit it.' People were saying to me, 'Have you lost your mind?' As a fundraiser in the fall, 2006, at an inter-squad game, we set the challenge. She threw three pitches; I made three strikes. It's amazing to me that a human being can throw a softball that fast."

Mickey Dearstone,
radio sports announcer,
Knoxville, Tennessee

asked, "What's the deal? Why don't you want to throw this? Explain it to me." I said, "The USA coach told me that I am too lateral. He said that I need to throw up and down more. And you know I am, because last year the curveball inside to the right-handed hitters was hitting them or getting hit for a home run. I can't control the break on it. It just moves too much, or it doesn't move at all when I try to control it." Karen said, "Okay, that makes sense. What about the screwball?" I said, "Well, the coach said I throw too much side to side. And I need to work up, down, and slow." She said, "Your change-up is not that good." And I said, "I know. I'm practicing." And she said, "Are you going to throw a drop ball?" I responded, "Well, yeah, I've been working on it. I just need to go all in on it and make it work." Karen said, "I don't know if I agree with everything you said. I agree with your curveball. You are right there. That's a good decision. But I don't know if it's a good idea to get rid of your screwball. But let's not make that decision today. Let's talk about it. And let it work itself out."

Power to Karen and Marty on this, and also to Ralph, for believing in me. They pulled me into the office the next day, and I thought, "Oh, shoot, I am in trouble." Every time they asked me into the office, that's what I thought. They asked me to explain the whole situation. I said, "When I was at world championships, the coach talked to me, and he said this and this and this pitch is really good. And my rise ball is great, but I need something that is lower in the zone. The screwball doesn't move enough. And the curveball—I hit the batters on. So I need to go up and down more." I was telling them this. Finally I had learned how to put words to my pitching. The tone of the conversation had changed from our freshman year disagreement. The mutual respect and information were there.

Marty called me for an individual practice and said, "I talked to Karen about this. We talked to your USA coaches and all that and this is what we think. We understand what you are trying to do. And we understand why you want to do it. If you are not going to throw these other two pitches, you'll have to be able to throw your rise for a strike. But are you willing to learn something new? Are you willing to give this a try? If it doesn't work, we will go back to the other thing." So I scheduled an individual workout with Marty. That's when he showed me. He said, "I played men's fastpitch, and they did this. And my dad has done it. We have seen it done before. In the past, they thought most women could not do it because they were not strong enough. Or that they didn't have the form for it. I think you are strong enough to be able to do this. It might take a little bit to get it. But I think you can handle it." I'll never forget. He said, "Here is the thing, though: with this pitch you are going to get a ton of strikeouts. But if you leave it or it doesn't break, it is going to get hit hard. You are going to give up a home run every now and then because it doesn't break as much as the normal rise. People might sit on it. I think that is a risk we are willing to take because you have your other rise, and we can mix zones and levels better. We will be okay with it."

So we went out to the mound. It was sunny midday. And he taught me how to throw the low rise. The low rise goes from your knees to your belly button. Your normal rise is probably thigh to head. Those were two different pitches. And that is important to note. When I was pitching, I was able to pick up the low rise so well because we differentiated it from the normal rise. We almost made it a new pitch. It got its own sign. It got its own location. It got its movements and identity. We knew the purpose of this pitch versus the purpose of the normal rise ball. Is it basically the same pitch with tweaks in your body and mechanics? Yes, it's pretty much the same, but the way we executed it, talked about it, and gave it its own identity was completely different. And I think that helped me develop it. It helped me separate levels on a rise ball.

It wasn't like Marty taught me some significant new thing. It was more that he helped me mold what I was already doing. He showed me how to use what I was doing. No one had ever done that before. It was groundbreaking to me. It really changed the game for me because people were trying to read the rise ball spin to not swing at it—and then it was a strike or then it was a ball. And they were swinging at balls. Then the hitter could not tell the difference between the heights or levels of the pitches.

Tennessee went back to the World Series that year. We were so excited. We had been waiting for the World Series all year. We were pumped up. We believed we were so much better than everyone. "This is it. We can do this, ladies!" We felt like this was the year we were going to win.

Four-time All-American and NCAA strikeout record-holder, Tennessee's Monica Abbott pitches a rise ball in collegiate action. Courtesy of the University of Tennessee Athletics Department.

In the very first game of the World Series, we played Texas A&M. I was al-most too hyped—too excited. I walked the first three batters on eight straight balls. No hits; just balls, and then a strike and three balls. If you ever looked at my stats or know Tennessee softball, you know that I, in general, do not walk people. I don't give up a lot of free bases. Ralph and Karen were pretty adamant about that—you don't walk people. I remember the timeout: Marty came out and he said, "Geez, Monica, take a deep breath. Snap out of it and go strikeout the next three batters." I dug myself into the deepest hole and that's what I did. I struck out the next three batters.

My senior year I dominated in strikeouts. It was a thing. Up until then I had 500 strikeouts every year, and my freshman year I was one of the first to do it. I don't think anyone has done it since then. I had 724 strikeouts my senior year—an NCAA single-season record that still stands. It was a 200-strikeout jump in one year. I did give up some home runs, but it was not as bad as we had thought it might be.

I came almost full circle, now that I think about it, between that terri-ble incident on the field my freshman year and my conversation with Karen during that senior-year scrimmage. The growth, empowerment, and trust were there for both of us, and having Marty there to help me was so import-ant. I could finally verbalize why I wanted to throw a certain pitch: this is what it feels like, and this is what I need. I thought it would help our team. And I thought it would help me achieve a step in my Olympic dream.

The University of Tennessee softball stadium opened the year after I graduated. I did get to play in it, because Team USA did a tour across the US in 2008. That was the first time I got to play in that stadium. I remem-bered during my college years watching fans lining up on the highway, blocking traffic, peeking between the windscreens, and lining up across the fence to see the games at Tyson Park where we played. On that day I knew that those same fans had seats in a new stadium. It was surreal to play in a USA uniform and to play in the stadium argued for and built because of the success of the Tennessee softball program when I was there. That is a day I will never forget.

"Monica Abbott put softball on the map at Tennessee. She wanted the challenge. You can credit Monica Abbott with the Sherri Parker Lee Stadium."

Mickey Dearstone, radio sports announcer, Knoxville, Tennessee

"I never got to meet Monica. But on the mound she was really focused. Her stare reminded me of Pat Summitt at Lady Vol basketball games."

Les Reed, Lady Vol fan

On March 23, 2013, the University of Tennessee retired my jersey, the first softball jersey retirement in Tennessee history. It's a big deal to be the first one. It was an incredible experience. My family was out there with me. Old teammates came out. The Lady Vols were actually playing Texas A&M, too—in a big spring game. I was playing in Japan at the time, and I came back in the middle of the season to go to the jersey retirement. It was special.

We had a big reception before the game with all of the older players. The stadium was still pretty new at that time. The president of the university was there. Ralph and Karen were there. I think Ivy and Ellen Renfroe* were still there, too. There were even some faculty there that I knew from the College of Communications. There were a couple of professors from college who had followed me and had come to my games. One of my professors had a daughter, and after I was in his class, they came to the games together. The sports information department and the sports medicine department came out. The daughter of one of the Scrap Yard Dawgs owners was the catcher for Texas A&M, so they were there when my jersey was retired, too. That same daughter, Megan May, was catcher on the national team. I wore jeans, a restricting Tennessee orange blazer, and wedge shoes. When I threw out the first pitch, the catcher missed it, and it hit the camera.

*From Jackson, Tennessee, sisters, Ivy (2011–2014) and Ellen (2010–2013) Renfroe, were pitchers for the University of Tennessee Lady Vol Softball team.

SIX REACHING MY OLYMPIC DREAM

In high school, I made the junior national team. We went to Hermosillo, Mexico. I did well on that team, and there was a lot of hype around me. When they had tryouts for the 2004 national team in November, I was not invited. I was thinking, "Why did I not get invited? At the junior nationals, I was named MVP." I asked Ralph Weekly to try and find out why I wasn't invited. They said that I was too young. I was eighteen and young for my class.

In 2005 I got invited to the national team tryouts in January. And I swear that I just mowed everybody down. I was throwing GAS! All these famous stars were there, and I didn't say a word to anyone. I think I threw a no-hitter, probably only throwing rise balls, in three appearances. It was the timing: tryouts were in early January, and that timing is tough. I struck out a lot of people. So, I made the team in 2005. That was my first time. I was on the team with returning Olympians Jennie Finch, Cat Osterman, and Crystl Bustos, along with two other younger pitchers they were looking at. I didn't play much—hardly at all. I was just on the team.

Then they invited me back to try out again in 2006. And I thought, "Gosh, I want to; I am all about being on the bench and cheering, but I want to play." My Olympic dream was to win. I went to the tryouts and the same exact thing happened. I struck out everybody. There may have been one hit off of me. So I made the team in 2006, and it was the same situation as the year before. Jennie Finch and Cat Osterman were on the team, as were a couple of other pitchers they were trying out: a five-person roster of pitchers. That's when I think I was starting to come into my own. It was a world championship year. They started to give me more responsibility. I got a few more starts. I played well. I worked my way up. We won the world championships. I didn't pitch in the finals. I just pitched in the pool play. I helped the team in general, but I was not the ace.

The next year, 2007, was my senior year in college. Tryouts were in January again, and it was the same kind of thing. I shut everybody down. I don't know if the difference was the coaches or the players, but that was the year the mindset changed. I wasn't just on the staff; all of a sudden, Monica could carry her own—or maybe they were testing me. We played in the Pan American Games and toured to play the professional teams. We had a lot of head-to-head scrimmages that year. I did really well. I got to pitch against the better teams.

Tryouts for the 2008 Olympic team were in the fall for the tour. I remember being a little concerned about whether I was going to make the team and whether I would be on the roster, because Lisa Fernandez was the GOAT of GOATs. She is the greatest. They were not going to cut Jennie or Cat; they had been on the 2004 team along with Lisa. There may have been one spot available if they took four or five pitchers. They said they would announce the results on Monday to the team at 10:00 a.m. by email and to the media at 11:00 a.m. I went home, and Monday morning I grew more and more anxious. I checked at 10:00 a.m.—nothing. At 10:01 a.m., I saw the email in my box. I thought, "Oh, please let me make it!" I opened the message and shouted to my family who were assembled in the dining room, "I made it!" We all hugged and cheered. What a moment that was!

They took three pitchers—Jennie, Cat, and me! The Olympic team roster only takes fifteen players. They took me over Lisa because they thought Lisa wasn't ready, I guess. I don't know. They made that choice in April, and the Olympics were in July. I just kept thinking about my dreams to pitch the Olympic Gold Medal Game and to celebrate with the team. I had this vision in my mind, and I was so ready for that. So that is how I prepared every single day. I did these crazy mock lineups for games and mock situations and workouts. I had a little tribe of people to help me, and Keith Berg was one of them. He was pretty creative. Preparing for the Olympics, we made fake rosters. We did these workouts when I would pitch an inning and then I would do things like burpees and shuttle exercises. We did a swimming workout that was really tough. We did a lot of pitching circuits. It was done mostly in a bullpen. We would be trying to make it as game-like as possible and raise the intensity of it to simulate what you might feel at the Olympics. The goal was to be so tired pitching-wise that it would feel easy at the Olympics. We did these workouts that made practice so challenging that the games would feel effortless.

Monica showcases her USA jersey, Silver Medal, and "perfect game" game ball from the 2008 Beijing Olympic Games.

By the time we got to the Olympics, I was so ready to go. We made some fun Olympic memories: Word got out that the US softball team brought a Wii Nintendo game, and we drew NBA players and other athletes to our living area for fun. Also, Beijing is known for its bad traffic, and on one of our game days, our bus got caught in it. Even though there was an Olympics lane, we arrived just fifteen minutes before game time. We only had twenty-five minutes to warm up! We were in a huge panic, but it all worked out.

Eight teams were in the Olympics. Jennie pitched the first game, and our team did really well. They let me have an inning to get the nerves out. Then Cat and I pitched most often. I pitched to the Netherlands, and I threw a perfect game—no hits, no score, first and only in Olympic history, still to this day.

In the head-to-head pool play rounds, we played Japan. The coaches put Cat in to start, but then they panicked and told me I was pitching the game. They thought it was going to be Cat versus one of their aces to pitch, but Japan didn't enter their ace. The coaches entered the change at the start of the game, and I had ten minutes to warm up. I was rushed. It was nerve-racking, but I ended up pitching phenomenally.

We played Japan in the semifinals to go to the championship game. And so, I pitched this game. It was a pretty tight game. It was 1–0, really close. I was doing great. They were getting more hits than they had in other games, but not many. We went into extra innings—nine innings in the semifinal game. We scored two in the ninth. Then their runner started at second and they ended up scoring one run in a tie-break. The coaches took me out and put Cat in, and we ended up winning the game. The big question was who was going to start in the finals.

They started Cat in the gold medal game. We went down early, 2–0. The coaches took her out after the scoring and put me in around the fourth inning when she got in trouble. When I came in, there were two errors behind me. There was a throw to second base, and they dropped the ball. And they ran a squeeze play, and there was an error there, too.* We ended up losing 3–1. It was our defense that hurt us.

After the Olympics, I was obviously a little disappointed, even depressed. I had this dream of being a gold medalist and the starting pitcher. It took me a while to get over that. I also had a lot of questions about why they didn't start me. I had prepared. I did everything I could to have started. And they just didn't choose me. You can't change it, but I had a lot of thoughts like that. What could I have done differently? I think it was one of the most talented teams we have had. We just couldn't pull it off. There was a lot of pressure on the US team because it was the last Olympics that we knew of for softball. They were blaming Team USA, saying, "Oh, team USA is too good. They win everything." There was a lot of that in the media.

I think a lot of people felt that I was the better pitcher at the time. It was kind of controversial. I was pitching so well. I was holding this Japanese team. And the team was playing really well behind me. A lot of people believed that I should have pitched, and I was more prepared and ready. When I look back, I understand. Our head coach at the time had a set plan for the

---

*In the judgment of the official scorer, an error is committed when a fielder fails to convert an out on a play that an average fielder should have made. A sqeeze play is executed when the runner on third base starts for home as soon as the pitcher starts the motion to pitch and the batter bunts.

quad, which was four years. It was Cat Osterman's time. We were preparing for her. I was the person that had to cover for her—so that Japan did not get looks at her or she wasn't tired. It was already a set plan. I was more like the guard or protector. I ate up all the innings so that Cat could pitch the gold medal game. But the controversy was that I was pitching out of my mind. I was hot, hot, hot, and Japan was really struggling to hit off of me because I was so hot. I loved the Beijing Olympics. A lot of Tennessee people and a lot of my hometown people came to Beijing. Playing for the USA was a great experience. I was one of three rookies on the team. Everyone else was a veteran. And I remember telling Jess Mendoza at the end of the games, "Let's get all the teams together for a picture to appeal for 2016." So, Jessica Mendoza, Stacey Nuveman, and I got Australia and Japan together with the message, "Put softball back into the Olympics."

Following the 2008 Olympics we made a lot of US guest appearances, including on the Oprah Winfrey Show, at the Women's Sports Foundation, and at the White House. I also did a post-Olympic tour around the southeast attending softball events and putting on clinics. I think I did a first pitch at the Tennessee Smokies baseball game—then dropped the puck for the face-off at the Knoxville Ice Bears hockey game. I even went to Ripley's Believe It or Not and did something with them in Gatlinburg. It was a really big deal to be celebrated, and I felt a lot of pride in our team.

At first, I had been very disappointed, but as time went by, I realized that I really had no regrets. I felt that I had done everything I could have done. I pitched my heart out. I fulfilled my role. I did everything they had asked me to do, and I had done it well.

In 2020, I expected things to be different. The Olympics were held in 2021 because of the COVID-19 pandemic. There were a lot of questions about how we could prepare for competition because of the pandemic. A lot of the games we were to play with All-Star or college teams were cancelled because the crowds were not allowed, or we weren't allowed on college campuses. We did not play that many games. There was not a pre-season. My challenge was finding live hitters to get in-game or situational experience before the games. I trained a lot harder. I was leaner and stronger. I was working on my pitches. I did everything I could to try to prepare. I was trying to talk with and share my international experience with my catchers a lot. The knowledge I had about these teams versus the knowledge they had was entirely different. Trying to mesh those two was important to me. We needed to get inside each other's brains a little bit.

Japan put on a really great event. They had added sections to their stadium, and it was unfortunate that they could not have fans, because the entire stadium would have been full.

In some ways I feel like history just repeated itself at the 2020 Olympics.

I pitched winning games against Canada and Australia. I expected to start in the finals. I figured anyone following our team leading up to the Olympics could see which pitcher was number one, two, three, four, and who was pitching well. It wasn't an epic battle or anything.

But the coach started Cat Osterman. Ally Carda and I were in relief. The coach said he was going to put me in during the next inning, but he let Carda go back out instead. I was hot and ready, and that's when he iced me. Carda got in trouble in the top of that inning when she went out. He then tried to put me in, and I was trying to get back up—I had not been warming up. When I went in, we were already in the toughest situation. I have never been so frustrated. It was really hard to understand, because if we were going to go into extra innings, we could always re-enter our starter. If the coach takes a reliever out, he cannot put the reliever back in. You've got to keep the reliever in.

Our team struggled offensively. We put too much pressure on ourselves. We were playing tight press instead of relaxed. I think we wanted it too much.

I think not having the crowd was an element, too—not having your family there. The Tokyo Olympics, the only one for softball—I don't know how it is going to go down in history, but there is definitely going to be a component about that. The Olympic Games is such a big deal in an athletic journey—for sports people in general, whether you are a supporter, player, or staff. You work in

> "We talked about her playing for the USA against Japan where she has played pro ball. She knew that the US and Japan were the biggest rivals in Olympic softball. She said that she hoped a few people in Japan would clap for her."
>
> John Devine, sports director, *Monterey Herald*

With Jennie Finch during the 2010 World Championships. Jennie was a great leader and friend to Monica.

sports, and for them to not have anyone there, it was sad. This is something that happens once in a person's career for a lot of people. Without a crowd, the human element was lost—the human touch that the Olympics is known for. It made everything impersonal.

What was cool, though, was what happened when I came home. The contrast of coming from the extreme COVID-19 world to a country full of fans was amazing. They had watched us! The Giants had me out for a first pitch with forty thousand people in the stands cheering for Monica. They were going crazy! My neighborhood had a party. I was celebrated at the 49ers' game. And then I had several parties with different organizations in the area.

A lot of people really supported me. If 2008 was about my personal athletic experience, then 2020 was more about how I was able to bring people along on the journey with me. I feel like more people were invested in me as an athlete and me as a person even though they were not able to be there. I probably could have done a tour of Olympic celebrations, because so many people wanted to do that. Overall, it was a good experience, and I am glad I went back and was able to play with that team. I have a lot of good friends and memories from the 2020 games.

There are a lot of different theories about why softball was not included in the 2012 and 2016 games. In the time frame that it was voted out (2003–2006), we were on the Olympic docket. They say it was voted out for a couple of reasons. It has a lot to do with the steroid era in baseball and also with MLB not sending top players to play. It was not really about the game of softball itself.

One problem was that baseball and softball don't really share facilities. In 2004 they built a new softball stadium in Athens. Softball is not a popular sport in Greece, so after the Olympics, no one ever used it. It cost one million dollars to build and just became wreckage.

Think about the time frame. Women's sports weren't getting covered that much. They were just hanging on the coattails of other things. Even today, with the advancement of technology, YouTube, Instagram, streaming, etc., women's sports still do not get wide coverage. Sometimes technology has been helpful because of the accessibility of information it provides. People are posting drills and information, how to call, and even highlight reels from college softball. When I post something on Instagram about a play in my game, people are seeing that, and the more you see, the easier it is to try to duplicate it, learn from it, or imitate it. That is helping other countries to be better and become successful.

I think technology is helping us in today's age a lot, but back when softball was voted off the Olympic docket, none of that was really available. Once we were voted off, we became a bid sport, meaning we had to appeal for votes for each Olympic Games. Now we come into competition with other sports bidding for one spot or two spots—sports that want to have a new Olympic sport presence—or a sport that is popular in the host country. For example, in 2016, it was important to London to have rugby in the games. So we went head-to-head with rugby, and rugby is a world sport—South Africa, India,

Brazil, Australia, New Zealand. In the southern hemisphere it is really popular. Going head-to-head with rugby was not ideal for softball.

Paris is hosting in 2024 in Europe, a continent not strong in softball. We do play there; for example, Netherlands has a strong team. Italy has been to every Olympics in softball. Great Britain has a team. The Czech Republic has a team. But softball is not really played in France. We had to go head-to-head with skateboarding. It is just difficult for countries that don't play this sport when you think about the venue and the cost of the Olympics. Paris would have to put in a baseball and a softball stadium. So that is two venue costs or one venue accommodating both sports, if they could pull it off.

Softball not being in the Olympics definitely affected me in 2012 and 2016. I think in 2008 people played because they thought it was going to be the last one. Then in 2020, there were people who had been playing and hoped they would have a chance to go to the Olympics.

The mental health of athletes is coming more into public focus. The pressure of competition is not so much an issue; athletes thrive on pressure—intense, high-pressure situations. That's what they train for. But in certain instances, when you build something up so much, it can have a negative mental effect on people—especially when things are unexpected or random things happen. This can stem from expectations of other people. Our society doesn't know how to deal with people who come in second place. You could lose by a quarter of a second or even be clearly in second place, and you are still better than 98 percent of the entire world. Some people see it as losing second place, silver medal, and winning third place, bronze medal.

In my case, I would say after the 2020 Olympic Games, I definitely struggled mentally. And I struggled mentally because of what happened when decisions out of my control were made. I was in a position where I was expected to be the ace by everyone on the team—every player—even the player that started. For something like that to happen, the way I was treated, the history, all of it—it's hard to wrap your mind around. Then having to go on to normal life after that is difficult. You have to talk about it. People keep wanting to talk about it.

Take Simone Biles at the 2020 Olympics: I would connect her case to the yips.* She had a place where she didn't feel safe competing in that event. There was a safety issue there. However well she was doing in her practices, I think that is what happened. I think if an athlete doesn't feel safe in their environment or safe in being able to perform, that can be a scary thing. I don't think it's a pressure thing; I think it's more that athletes struggle because we always talk about winning and competing and doing great and achieving your dreams. But what happens when something is completely out of your control? That's what happened to me. Twice.

I watched history repeat itself. I knew it was happening, and there was nothing I could do about it. Before the game started, I said, "History can't repeat itself. I am scared right now. What can I do? I can't do anything. You put the ball in my hand, I can do something. You can put the ball in someone else's hand that I know is ready to go. Or define how the roles are going to fit for people, your specific role on a team. We get that. But when something is thrown out of the blue moon, because you think you are being tricky or something, we don't get that."

When the roles are not established, it is difficult for people.

Athletes are on the public stage. We are expected to act and perform in certain ways all the time. It isn't always easy to separate life issues from sport. If athletes need to take a break because of personal issues, they risk criticism. They risk disappointing fans. We prepare for the pressure of competition. It's more difficult to handle the things in life we can't control. We all need time to regroup, consider priorities, and take care of all the aspects of our lives. Your mom is sick; you are late on a school paper, and you are going to fail; you are not allowed to show that on the field. That's our culture. I think it is good that athletes are beginning to speak up about this. The mind-body connection is true for all of us. The more we understand mental health, the more balanced and successful we will be.

---

*In sports, the yips are a sudden loss of ability to execute certain skills in experienced athletes. This condition may be caused by a neurological disorder, performance anxiety, or a mix of both.

SEVEN GOING PRO—A WHOLE NEW BALLGAME AND A MILLION-DOLLAR ARM

After my senior season, 2007, I went on to the national team for camps and tryouts. National Pro Fastpitch (NPF), the professional women's softball league in the United States, had a draft, but they said they didn't want to take any Olympic players because they would only be available for half the season since the USA and NPF seasons overlapped. Because of this, I thought nobody would draft me, but in the end I became one of the Washington Glory's last picks in the final round. Isn't that wild? I was leading the country in every statistical category. In 2007 I finished softball at the University of Tennessee, I played pro, and I did Team USA that summer. I played professional league and two or three pro events, including their championship events and series.

Then in the spring of 2008 Team USA was on tour, and we went to the Olympics. The following fall, I took one more class and completed my degree at the University of Tennessee. I really didn't do much—it was post-Olympics, so I just hung out. Sometimes I would go help the Lady Vol softball team. I did a bunch of post-Olympic tour events and events that my agency set up—camps and clinics around Tennessee and across the southeast.

I had the option to go to Toyota, but I didn't know if I wanted to do that. We had just lost to Japan in the Olympics; they were our rivals, and it was frowned upon. USA management advised against going. I was the youngest player on the 2008 Olympic team. There wasn't a lot of guidance at that point—or opportunities. I was conflicted because softball wasn't in the 2012 Olympics. We already knew it was voted out. And we had an older US team: all of our bigger stars were either done or only going to play one or two more years. Now what? What are you going to do now, Monica?

Natasha Watley, who played shortstop on Team USA with me, was thinking the same way. She thought it would be cool if she could play in Japan. But she needed a pitcher to be able to play. I had three or four offers from different teams, and I was dragging my feet to make a decision. I talked to Tasha about it multiple times. We were pretty good friends already. Lisa Fernandez said to me during training camp once, "Monica, why don't you just go for one or two years and make a little money and come home?"

I took the best offer I had. If I was going to make money, I wanted to win. Most people brought catchers. But my catcher, Shannon Doepking, was still in college, so I couldn't take her with me. And the national team catchers were retiring. I had a couple of other choices of catchers to take, but I was concerned. I don't hit. We couldn't win if we didn't score. I needed somebody who could help us score and help us win. That was my strategy. Why not go with Tash? She could hit .550; she could do multiple things. And we got along well. That was my thought. I was going to take the best offer and see if they would take Tash with me. In December 2008 I signed with Toyota to play in the 2009 season, and I was thinking, "Okay, let's go for one year—maybe two. And I could still do the US pro league."

In spring 2009, while I was in Japan, the Washington Glory ended up folding, and the USSSA Pride, a fastpitch team in Florida, bought them out. I came back from Japan and signed a year-long NPF contract to play with the Pride that summer. In 2009 the Pride was not very good—we were thrown together—but we ended up getting to the finals in the championship! We were last place in the regular season, had a strong run, and made it to the championship game. We ended up losing and coming in second place.

The Pride was really new, and we were trying to figure out a system that worked. Teammates Kelly Kretschman, Caitlin Lowe, and I tried to see how we could get players to play longer and make it more of a full-time job, so it wasn't such a hustle. At that time women's sports were still struggling to be seen on TV for that exposure. Social media wasn't that big of a deal yet, with just Facebook and a little bit of Twitter. Most softball athletes at that time retired by age twenty-five. They would coach a college team and they would play in the summer. They would be a graduate assistant while they were getting their master's degree after they stopped playing with their college. And then they would stop playing altogether. I talked with the Pride about these issues. They liked our ideas.

We went to work to design strategies that would attract and retain other athletes. We developed a playing contract and marketing contract that included clinics, appearances, and work that players could do year-round to represent the Pride. Next, we worked to recruit our players, teammates to make this team better. In the winter and early spring, we started recruiting all of our friends. We knew we had to get people we wanted on this team. It was time to get better athletes. So, we got our friends from the Olympic team on the team. We asked Jess Mendoza and Andrea Duran if they wanted to play. It was a little bit better with the marketing contract—more ideal.

I returned to Japan in March 2010. I got Tash to come to the Pride in spring 2010. I got all my friends to come to the Pride—convinced them to come. I even got Shannon Doepking to come to the Pride. But management didn't like that I was in Japan. No one liked it, but they never said it to me up front. It was a rumor.

At the first of May, when the team was all set for summer season, they traded me to the Tennessee Diamonds for Cat Osterman. I learned this in a two-line email: "We traded you to the Tennessee Diamonds." That is all it was. I tried to call them, and they ignored me.

At that point I was kind of mad. I helped build them. I helped them go from last place to second place in the championships. I felt shafted. I had worked to set up a playing contract and marketing contract. I had helped recruit my Olympic team. I wasn't the only one involved, but I worked a lot to set that up. I was at the base of it.

I went from an organization that had a playing contract and a marketing contract to the Tennessee Diamonds, a team where I wasn't even getting paid. I think I made $1,500 that summer. The team was owned by the league, so there wasn't an individual owner.

Our jerseys were bad. They just didn't have it together. We would show up at the airport and there would be no cars rented. We thought, "If they don't respect us, why should we try so hard?" These were things that no professional athlete should ever have to deal with. It was worse than the baseball minor leagues. Management didn't think about it that way. We were just transactions to them.

I wouldn't say that I am an emotional person, but my heart has to be in it for me to perform well. I didn't want to be there. My mentality wasn't "let's go play to win." I did my own thing. I didn't talk to a lot of people. I got mad. I got mad at some of my teammates who helped start the Pride. I got mad at the league. I felt like I had gotten the short end of the stick. My mind was out of the game, and my heart was out of it, too. I think the only reason I ended up playing that season was that it was in Nashville, Tennessee, and my college friends were living in Tennessee at that time. I spent most of my time with them.

Monica discussing game strategy with teammate Miu Goto during a Toyota Red Terriers game. Goto would become the youngest player on the Japanese Olympic Team in 2021.

Surprisingly, 2010 ended up being a blessing in disguise. I had a great summer that year. It was a lot of fun. Some of the girls on that team are still some of my close friends. We didn't have a good year in softball, mostly because the team structure was not organized. But I think it created balance for me because I started to play with people who valued the balance of life more. They knew softball wasn't everything. They loved to compete. They were good athletes. But they knew their time was coming to an end on the softball field— and they were okay with it. It helped me to see that, too. It made me think about why I play. Why is it important for me to play? Why am I doing this? Looking back on it now, I think this experience showed me a lot about professional sports and also gave me a lot of perspective around what I wanted and what I didn't. I was forced to balance softball and life and realized that I had to find something to do business-wise. This helped me as a person.

In the softball world a lot was going on. Media people didn't know where to put their marketing dollars. Softball was out of the Olympics again. The pro league in the United States wasn't doing so well. There were just four teams. I was on the one owned by the league. Think about it from their side:

it just wasn't an ideal situation. After that I said, "I don't think I want to play in the NPF. I'm just going to do Japan."

So, I went back to Japan, and we won our first championship in the fall of 2010. And then things started to come together on the professional side. Toyota won back-to-back-to-back championships (2010, 2011, 2012). I was so tunnel-visioned through college and the Olympics, and now going to Toyota so tunnel-visioned on pitching and performing, that I didn't really have the chance to soak things in.

In January 2011, the Diamonds folded. The Chicago Bandits reached out to me and asked me to come play for them. I had said I was not going to play in the NPF anymore. I just didn't think it was for me. So when the Bandits called and asked me to play, I said I didn't think I would. I was going to play in Japan for Toyota and maybe do Team USA. They kept messaging me and wanting me to play. They were very upfront. They said, "Jennie retired. This is who is on our staff right now. We are not looking for you to replace Jennie Finch. We are looking for you to start your career with the Bandits. You have gotten the short end of the stick professionally so far. The Bandits are the oldest NPF team. We think you will have a good following here. You can find a home with the Chicago Bandits." I really liked that. It took a lot of stress off of me. You can't replace Jennie Finch. I loved Jennie. If Jennie Finch built the Bandits, I was more than happy to carry her torch forward. I thought, "Yeah, I can pitch after her—carry the torch forward for her. I would love to do that, do what I can to continue her legacy forward with that organization." I said that I would come but wanted Shannon Doepking to come with me.

In 2011, the Bandits opened the first women's professional softball stadium in Rosemont, Illinois, on 27 Jennie Finch Way. I got to open the stadium with Jennie throwing out the first pitch. Shannon was there. We both got to experience that together. We won the championship with the Bandits, and life was good. That year is when my professional career started to have some guidance and direction.

It was as they said. We got to start new traditions at the stadium. The fans and the atmosphere were incredible. They really did take to me. They

Monica (*back row, right of center*) with her Chicago Bandits professional teammates in 2016 after a perfect game.

became big fans of mine. And to this day, the Bandits Nation is very into what I am doing. They are very avid fans. I had some really good years there. I threw some perfect games. I broke the speed record (seventy-seven mph) in the Guinness Book of World Records, and I was in a Bandits uniform.

It really started to show that when you put someone in a positive environment and an atmosphere that enables them to succeed, they'll go above and beyond. That's what happened to the Bandits and me. I was put into a great atmosphere and environment with people that were trying to do the best they could for the sport. And the Bandits started to thrive.

We probably over-performed for our talent level. We became epic rivals with the USSSA Pride, the team that traded me. Remember, I had recruited all of my friends for the Pride. My friends were on that team, but we could beat them. Our games were exciting. I pitched in the beginning. We had a couple of people that could compete, but they couldn't really hold their own against the Pride. We would play one game really well. And then the next one we would lose 10–1. And then we would play game three in the series, and pitch by commission meaning that everyone on the team is going to pitch that day. A pitcher would stay in for as long as they could, and then I would come in to close. We would try to win 2–1 or 3–2.

We had a really good overall atmosphere and team. I lived ten minutes from the stadium. They put us all in city housing that was nearby. People lived pretty close to one another, too. We had little apartments, and it became a lot of fun. I played with Tammy Williams and Amber Patton, who are still good friends of mine to this day. We won several championships, and we made a ton of memories in Chicago during the summer. We went to Lake Shore Drive. We went to the Willis Tower. We rented a boat and went out on the lake. We would have fireworks at the stadium and do movies there sometimes. We did a lot of events and activities. We partied hard, and we played hard, with so many fun things to do in Chicago.

When I played for the Bandits, I started to get involved in life outside of playing with the team. That's when I started being more personable with fans. I was involved in more activities like first pitches for kids. We had a golf outing that I was involved in. I would do some volunteer work—things like that. That's when I got more involved on the community side in initiatives with the Bandits rather than just playing.

People thrived there because we were allowed to be ourselves, and I think part of it was the way management treated people. That environment wasn't just for me; it was a healthy environment for everyone. It allowed us to play at our best, it motivated us to win—we wanted to be involved and successful. We would have ideas, such as, "Oh, we have this scoreboard. We should make a hype video. Then Tammy Williams, Amber Patton, Danielle Zymkowitz, and I made a hype video. We didn't have someone to do it, so we said, "Let's do it ourselves!" We needed a place to work out. We found a place we liked, and all of a sudden, they became our workout sponsor. We got the community involved.

It was the kind of atmosphere where we felt we could make an impact on an organization. People were invested. All of us were really invested in it. We created a little fan club group on Facebook called "Bandit Nation." We said, "How about if you guys do a barbeque after the game?" So we got post-game meals, and we would go up there and talk about the game with this group of fans that came to all of our games. There was a couple who would make moonshine and bring it to this upgraded tailgate atmosphere. They said, "You went to Tennessee, so we made moonshine." Afterward, we signed autographs and mingled with the fans.

"In her long career, Monica has stayed on top in every part of the game."

Jennie Finch, All American and US Olympic Pitcher

This environment generated a work hard, play hard spirit. I think we were playing a four-game series. One of the games was a night game, so the teams had to stay over. Both teams were out, and people seeing us were saying, "Oh, you are the Bandits. We have heard about you." There was a couple among the fans who owned a party bus, and they would give us a discount to rent the bus at night. And we would have both teams go out to downtown Chicago. We loved that city, and we made other teams love it, too.

We made fans wherever we went. When we went to Starbucks, we'd say, "Come to our games; we'll give you a ticket." And then the Starbucks barista would show up and say, "Oh, here, we brought you some iced coffee." Shannon and I used to go to a health and fitness center. We went to a spin class at nine in the morning, where Sandy, a retired woman, ran the class. There would be five people in her class, and then the entire spin class would show up at our game.

In Chicago the Blackhawks are really big—ice hockey. Playing in Chicago, I did love the Blackhawks. They won a couple of years when we were there. We started talking about how the Blackhawks had a song at their games. The Cubs had a song. We needed our own song to play. For the longest time we couldn't come up with a song, so we decided that after each win they would play the Blackhawks song. It was awesome and so fun.

I remember in 2011 when we won the first game opening the new stadium. We were definitely not expected to win. When you looked at the Pride, player-to-player we didn't match up—a team of Olympians vs. the Bandits. We probably shouldn't have been winning, but we were. We had good chemistry. We had good teamwork. We were super feisty. We were very sassy on the field. We were a funny team.

One year, we had a pitcher named Nikki Nemitz. She had played for the University of Michigan. There were two pitchers who got recruited out of Michigan—one went to the Bandits; one went to the Pride. And they were playing head-to-head in a battle. Nikki was pitching really well, and we were chanting, "Our Michigan is better." We would make it a clap: "Our Michigan is better, clap, clap."

In 2011 after we won the championship, we got to bring the trophy home. In that day and age, players would leave and go home after a championship game. We actually got to bring the trophy home to Rosemont. We all went home to the stadium, put the trophy on home plate, and took a picture. Then we had a party with the fans.

Creating a good atmosphere and a healthy environment off the field made our team work that much better—and it was a lot more fun to play. We played pranks on each other a lot. One time, just before a two-week road trip, one of the girls put a "for sale" sign on Shannon Doepking's car with her phone number. During those two weeks, she was getting all these calls: "Is your Charger still available? What is your best offer right now? Would you take ten grand for it?"

We pranked our coaches, too. We covered their cars with mini post-it notes and filled their offices with cups of water. One time someone hit the fence, and we drew an outline of a body on the fence like a crime scene. We were entertaining, living in the moment.

In 2013 Shannon retired, so we needed a catcher. I convinced management to bring over my Toyota catcher, Kazuki Watanabe. I said, "Let's make the league international. We go over there; why don't you guys come over here?" I told management, "She's got to have someone to talk to, so you need to bring another player. Why don't we get Eri Yamada? She hit the winning home run in the 2008 Olympics against Cat Osterman. We know she can hit. She's still playing and has a name Americans would recognize." I was able to help facilitate some of the first Japanese players to come over and play for the Bandits. Then other people started to come as well. Overall, the core group was good and strong. People came in and out. Each year was a little bit different based on who was in charge and other people on the team, but the core values stayed the same.

Those Bandit years, 2011–2015, were the prime time for professional softball. That rivalry between the USSSA Pride and the Chicago Bandits was epic. Those games were incredible. They were probably some of the best games ever played, and I am not just saying that because I played for the Bandits. These games should have been on TV. There were a lot of highlights in my career during that time frame.

One time the Cubs asked me to come throw out the first pitch. You can bring two friends. I said, "First pitch, do you want me to come say hi to the players with my team before the game? And watch the game?" And they said, "Oh yeah, that's what we want." So the whole team went to pre-game batting practice, and we threw some pitches to some of their hitters.

I really think it was important to the overall environment that our core group—Tammy Williams, Amber Patton, Shannon Doepking, and I, plus a few others—started to build our own traditions. It became easy for this spirit to trickle down over the years. The standard and levels of traditions passed throughout the team and the organization as a whole. You could have all the talent in the world; you could have the most talented team, but if you don't have the teamwork or the chemistry or just the personality, whether that's in the team or the staff and the organization itself—that can affect either side. If the team's chemistry is not very good, that can affect how the staff wants to work for you. If the staff's chemistry isn't great, it's going to affect the team, because players are going to have to deal with a lot more distractions.

So many things came together. Having Shannon there was huge for me. Before signing with the Bandits, I didn't think I would ever want to play for the NPF again. I had still been searching for my own identity. The entire Chicago area supported the Bandits, too, just like the city of Rosemont, building that stadium. People mattered. I am so grateful I played in Chicago.

This is the type of organization we were in. There was an indoor training facility—a "bubble," so to speak—that had two softball fields and cages. It was a tent. One time we were playing a game at the stadium in the middle of July, and right at game time, there was a micro-burst storm. Rain poured with wind gusts of sixty mph with lightning and thunder for fifteen minutes straight. Our game in the stadium stopped. Everyone was cleared out and covered. The storm stopped, and everybody started walking back to the field. Glass from lights had shattered and was all over the field from the storm. And then the bubble popped, and the tent came down. A clinic had been going on inside that day. Everyone panicked that kids could be under there. Everyone on staff, everyone in the organization, started army-crawling underneath the tent—just to make sure there wasn't one kid or an umpire underneath. They didn't hesitate. They were the kind of people who ran into the fire to make sure that everyone was safe. A few players were running after them, and the coaches were saying, "No, you guys stay here!" They cleared that area, and then they cleared the tent. We players just started combing the field to pick up glass. The game was postponed, so we signed autographs and started to clean up the stadium. No one had to tell us to do that; we did it because that is what you do. We didn't expect anything. We just did it.

The humor on this team was unreal. Let's say I was throwing a perfect game. Then I would walk someone in the sixth inning. My teammates would say, "Gosh, Monica, a perfect game isn't good enough for you? You have to walk somebody and just get a no-hitter. Why settle?" They would say stuff like that. We broke through awkwardness and discomfort with humor.

Then there was Tammy Williams, our shortstop. She struck out sometimes. Then in one game, she had three strikeouts in a row, and she was coming up on her fourth time at bat. We said, "Oh, Tammy, you are 0–3 with three strikeouts. You currently have a hat trick in softball. If you get one more strikeout, you can go for the grand sombrero." Then of course she struck out, and our team showed up that night if we had a party or the next day in practice with a sombrero. We were so funny; we just killed ourselves with really bad humor. We didn't take ourselves too seriously, but we were serious about winning. We wanted to win. We had to have humor to stay serious and to be competitive. I think we had a great balance of on-off intensity. If we hadn't been able to joke and play pranks and party hard and work hard, all of this would not have been nearly as good an experience.

I definitely think a key to my success has been knowing when to turn it on and off—not just on the field but in life and in relationships. You can't run through life at a hundred miles per hour, living and dying off every success you have or don't have. You have to manage and balance it. I'm an intense person when I step on the mound. I love the intensity. I love being in tune with the moment, but then my team would make jokes and make it fun. I wasn't making the jokes, but I still wanted to laugh. In the game, I don't like to make jokes when I am pitching. But if someone else is making jokes, then I will laugh. When I am not pitching, then I make the jokes. I think they recognized that about me and respected that. It created a safe space for me to realize that, hey, I am actually pretty funny.

We were people who loved the game. We did not necessarily make more money than other teams. We didn't necessarily have all the big names—big sponsorships or anything like that. But in our own way we created a great environment that made it fun to play and fun for people to watch. It made it fun to be a professional. Some other athletes were probably a little jealous of that. We really cared. We cared about the success of the team. We cared about the success of each other.

After 2015, my last year with the Bandits, Amber Patton, our third baseman, retired. Tammy Williams, the shortstop, and I were on the same page; we were not sure we wanted to play again. We had been this trio. Tammy asked me before we went to the finals, "Are you going to play next year? What are you thinking?" And at that point in late summer I said, "No, I don't think I am going to play for the Bandits anymore." They had cut my salary that year. They were making a lot of budget cuts. The team was getting younger, and a lot of things were changing in the organization—nothing softball-wise, just with ownership and management. I had just turned thirty. And I was at the point where I was thinking I might just go and play for Toyota two or three more years and then call it. Or maybe if the Olympics came back, I would think about playing there.

I didn't need to keep playing a nine- or ten-month season. I was playing from late March to November. I wasn't getting that much off-time. In my position, I am the main person on the team. It is not like I can just be a con- tributor. I went March to June in Japan to play for Toyota and then came back to the NPF from June to August to play for the Bandits. The Japanese season takes a summer break. I would take a short break and then begin the summer season in the states. After the pro season, I would go back to Toyota for the fall season in November. I was playing basically a nine- or ten-month season for fourteen years. It was grueling. In my twenties, it was good for me. It was fun, and I enjoyed travelling.

Now I wanted to scale back and have some down time. My thought was that in the US, if I just played for Team USA, my schedule would be a little bit lighter. That was before the finals. Fall went by, and I went to Toyota. The next January came, and I was still planning to play for Toyota, because I wanted to get my ten years playing there. I think I had two more years to make the ten-year mark.

I was getting ready for that and training at home when Shannon Doepking texted me and asked, "Are you going to play for the Bandits this year? There is a team that wants you to play for them." I told her that I was thinking about not playing for NPF. She asked, "What do they have to offer to make you play?" I said, "I really don't want to play." I kept saying no. Then they start offering salaries. I kept saying, "No, I don't think so." Then the salaries started to get higher. I thought it was a joke. Shannon was at Dartmouth at that time, and I was her volunteer coach and working out to get ready for Japan. Shannon said, "These are great people, and they want to offer you a contract to play for them."

For about five years I had been playing in Japan and playing with the Bandits. Things were going really well—I was having a great time, and life was good. I started building my Abbott Athletics business on the side. I was doing events across the country—speaking to groups, teaching, and pitching. I figured out my identity as a professional and what it takes to win. And then 2015 came and I was nearing thirty years old. I thought, "I am going to stop. This is going to be my last year of playing professionally in the states. I don't think I want to keep doing this nine-month season—unless it's an offer I can't refuse."

And then the women's empowerment movement began.

That is the time when women's soccer began their lawsuit against the federation that was officially filed in 2019.* Equal pay was a big thing and starting to gain traction in the news. The Scrap Yard Dawgs, a new team based in Houston, Texas, contacted me. I never said "send me a million-dollar contract" or anything like that. They asked me how much I needed to play—five figures, six figures. I just kept saying, "I love my time with the Bandits. I am not really interested in leaving them."

I was not interested in going to a first-year organization—experiencing that again. I didn't want to go through the Diamond situation again or my experience with the Pride. I was happy. I was going to continue playing in Japan and bow out quietly from the pro league. Those were my plans.

The Scrap Yard Dawgs kept asking, and I kept saying no. Finally I told them, "You will have to give me something I can't say no to, because I am not sure I want to go down that road again."

I returned to Japan as I had planned. I didn't have anything going on in the summer and had decided to take the summer off. In April the Scrap Yard Dawgs management flew to Japan for a meeting. They offered me one million dollars. I didn't think it was possible. I said, "Yeah, right, you aren't going to do that." I called their bluff, and I think that is why they came to Japan—to convince me that they were serious. And when it actually happened, I said, "Holy cow! Do I actually want to do this?" This was the highest-paying deal by a franchisee for any female athlete in a team sport in the history of US athletics. At that point I felt an obligation not only as an athlete but as a female athlete to agree to this contract that would send a message across the world

*In March 2019 the United States Women's National Soccer Team brought a class-action lawsuit against US Soccer, alleging gender discrimination that affected the pay scale between the men's and women's national teams. In 2022 US women's soccer stars reached a $24 million settlement with the US Soccer Federation.

to everyone. And then I had to call the Bandits and tell them I wasn't playing. I had to call my teammates and tell them what was going to happen. So, in 2016 I went to the Scrap Yard Dawgs. They owned a six-field facility. They had alcohol sales, and that was the big moneymaker.

I never thought that was going to happen. But I felt that it was my job and responsibility to carry the torch—to help create that opportunity not only for women in general but also for the sport of softball. I also knew I could carry that load. I had been around some of the most influential women in sports. I had meetings with Pat Summitt. I went to Tennessee, where my co-head coaches were paid the same (male and female). I had been to the Women's Sports Foundation and seen Billie Jean King. I got to see Jennie Finch build her career. I watched Lisa Fernandez, a phenomenal athlete and pitcher, not get the credit she deserves. She was a game changer for softball during her time. These players were so good already. They should have already had million-dollar contracts by the time I signed mine.

I was a face for professional softball at the time, and the conversation around pay equity was happening. It became public: it wasn't just between spouses or parents or daughters and parents. I have seen other incredible female athletes not receive the equitable treatment they deserved. So, I thought, "I can be a voice and at least a face for this." After the million-dollar contract with the Dawgs, noticed a lot of NCAA coaches stepped up and renegotiated their own contracts. In 2017 we won the championship. I ended up playing pro the whole summer.

I was with the Scrap Yard Dawgs in 2016, 2017, and 2018, and then late 2019 and 2020, things started to get a little unstable. They never fulfilled or completed the million-dollar contract. We didn't play in 2020 or 2021. In 2020 the NPF folded.

EIGHT   CALL ME "ABBO TO SAN"

In 2007 I was playing for the national team, and the leagues in Japan started asking me to go to Japan. I just kept saying, "No. My priorities are Team USA and finishing school." Then in 2008, Michele Smith, a left-hander, two-time Olympian, and All-American from Oklahoma State, was looking for someone to replace her at Toyota Shokki. I just wasn't ready to say yes. I needed to finish school. In the fall of 2008, several teams were inviting me to go to Japan. In the past, a pitcher and a catcher would always come together—so a foreigner pitcher and a foreigner catcher. But at the time, my US catchers were all older and not playing anymore. They had retired after 2008.

Shannon Doepking, whom I wanted to catch for me, still had a year of college left. There was one other person I could go with as a catcher, but I didn't know her very well. Being shy, I was concerned about going over to another country and having that be the only person I could talk to. I had several options with different teams in Japan, and most of them were with catchers.

Natasha Watley wanted to go, but as a shortstop, she could only go if she got a pitcher to go with her. I thought, "I know I can pitch, but I know I can't score any runs. I need somebody that can hit." I was looking at some of the options for catchers and thinking, "I don't know if they are good hitters." I knew Tasha could at least make something happen. She was good. I would rather go over there with someone who was going to hit .400 than take someone who could catch for me but not hit. I could teach someone to catch for me. As long as they could handle speed, I could work on the catching and the calling. I would figure that out. One thing I did know is that I needed to win.

Tash and I had played on the Olympic team and on Team USA together. We were friends, so I knew we would get along. And she was considered a triple threat: bunt, slap, hit. I thought, "Maybe I should go with Tash. I know we will have fun no matter how it turns out. Since I don't hit anymore, I can't go in and hit a home run to help us win. Tasha can do that. She hits home runs, and I strike people out. The hardest part will be trying to get the catcher." That was our mentality when Tash and I went to Japan. She said, "I know I can hit, but I can't keep them from scoring runs." They would only take her if she came with a pitcher. We partnered up.

Toyota ended up giving me a really nice offer, so I decided to take that and play for them. We both signed with the Toyota Red Terriers. It was a little bit controversial, because normally pitchers went with catchers. At that time, it was unheard of that a position player was coming. Tasha played shortstop for three or four years and then went into the designated hitter role, batting leadoff. We became this dynamic duo for eight years and won a lot together until she retired in 2017.

When we signed with Toyota, Japan had just won the gold medal in 2008. There were some feelings about that. Our mindset was, "Let's just see what they do and learn from them. Instead of giving information about how we do it, let's learn their way." I think in the beginning they were shocked, because they had not had that before. Usually, the foreigners would just come and do their practice and leave. They didn't know them that well. But we immersed ourselves in the team.

When I first arrived in Japan, I went through a pretty big adjustment period. I had to help mold a catcher for the team. It was 2009, and the world was a lot different, too. We were in a recession. Toyota was in the middle of the Prius recall. It was before FaceTime. The only thing we had was Skype—no texting. The world was a lot smaller in 2009 than it is today. I had to learn how to coach myself. That was also a big adjustment.

In Japan they learn English from a young age, from first grade and up, so they know English pretty well. I had a Japanese tutor. I took lessons. I am not fluent, but I am good enough to get by, and I am always trying to improve. It's fun. It is a complete challenge. I've had to learn how to laugh at myself. I say some of the stupidest things in Japanese via translation, and everyone starts laughing. And I'm saying, "What, what did I say? Why are you laughing at

Monica with catcher,
Kazuki Watanabe,
sharing pre-game
encouragement
early in her Toyota
Softball Career. The
two helped establish
a tradition for the
Toyota Red Terriers.

me?" Another language is hard, but I am trying. I've got a knack for it, and I might as well try to learn it. I think it is important to learn another language at a younger age. I wish I had learned Spanish from a younger age.

That first year was definitely a struggle. I came to Japan as a young pitcher with raw talent and skill, and while I had a lot of knowledge of the game, I hadn't been able to use it yet. I had a lot of growing to do as a businesswoman and an adult in Japan. It was a high-stress, high-intensity, performance-based environment. If you don't perform, they let you go and bring in someone else. It is not an atmosphere for your average college softball player. It is not for the weak of heart. A lot of people can't hang in with Japan because of how demanding they are. There are more competitive teams in Japan. They bring in foreigners so they can win.

The first year was so busy because we had everything thrown at us, and we had no idea what was going on. We were being shuttled everywhere. It was hard because of the language barrier, not being able to communicate what we wanted. I was not sure whether they understood me—we had to talk through an interpreter, which was something else we had to adjust to. I had to speak at the level of the interpreter's English.

That first year, in the middle of a finals game, there was a runner on base. It was an intense situation. The coach called timeout, and the interpreter looked nervous. She was panicking, and Tasha and I were saying, "What's she saying? What'd she say?"

All of a sudden, the interpreter looked at us and said, "Throw it to the higher bag." I think that was the interpretation. It was not proper English or proper softball vocabulary. She was a temporary interpreter. She didn't know anything about softball. Her English was good, but she had learned English in London. There are some differences with American English. So, we were in the middle of the most intense game. She said, "Throw it to the higher bag," and ran off the field. Tasha and I were still both standing on the mound saying, "What did she say?" I was thinking, "There is only one bag. Do we throw it above us? Throw the ball high? How is the second baseman going to catch it?" We were panicking because we were in an intense situation. Now I realize she was saying to get the lead runner out, to go for the double play. In the moment I didn't hear that. I had no idea what she was saying.

Overall, we had a good first year. We played really well. We won the league. We were ready to win and said, "Let's go see our Toyota president to thank him for the support." We went in to tell him that we were going to the final tournament, and our coach looked at me and said, "You have to ask him for something." I said, "Me?" They put me under pressure, and they all started staring at me in the office. "Can you come to the game?" I asked. The coach and team had wanted me to ask for a bus or upgrades to the field, something more physical. But he came to the game, and when he showed up, we started losing. We lost in the finals. He said, "Oh, no! I am bad luck. I shouldn't have come." Before Tasha and I came, our team had been middle of the pack. Now, our first year, we played in the finals for the championship. This was the first time we had been to the final tournament in years. It was a really big deal. Our president ended up falling in love with softball because he came to the game. Toyota softball was doing so well! We were the talk of the town.

We experienced things like prejudice because we weren't Japanese softball players. In the finals, we were winning, and one of their national team players was up to bat. It was a twenty-pitch at-bat because the umpire wouldn't call strike three. He just kept calling it a ball, and it was right down the middle—seriously, it was. After all these pitches, he walked the bases loaded. They used to do stuff like this just to show favoritism to their national team members or Japanese softball players. That was a lot to deal with, but somehow, we had fun and wanted to come back.

I had to tell our coach and the general manager at the end of the year that I couldn't come back if they didn't get a different interpreter, because she didn't understand softball or pitching. The education level wasn't there. The English level wasn't there. We needed someone who at least understood and knew the game. Tasha and I were afraid to tell them that. It's hard to say that to someone you work with every day. Maybe they wouldn't want us because we were too demanding.

The next year, 2010, we ended up getting a new interpreter. That is when it came together for Toyota. The overall communication was better, so the pitching and catching got a lot better. Again, we made it to the final tournament and met with the president to thank him for the support. This time I said, "They want me to ask you for a team bus." Our team was killing it. Everyone was really motivated. We were so close. And he came, and we won. He ended up falling in love with us because we beat our rival in the semifinal. And then in the finals, I ended up throwing a no-hitter in the first game. We won 3–0. It was a solid win. We scored in the third inning. It was good.

In our second (and last) game, we were head-to-head—0–0—Abbott versus Yukiko Ueno. Year in and year out, this was the Japan softball league: We were playing an international tiebreaker where they put a runner on second base in the top of the eighth. After seven innings if you can't score, it's a tiebreaker. We ended up playing ten innings.

I was pitching great. We were head-to-head—lots of strikeouts—all the things. They bunted it back to me, and I made a bad throw overhand to first base. The runner scored, and the next runner ended up on second base. They ended up getting two runs. I got out of the inning. I thought it was over. I was devastated. I was pacing in the back and thinking, "Monica, you idiot. You dummy."

But we were the home team, so we had our chance to bat in the bottom of the inning in the tiebreaker. There was no way we were going to score two runs. How could this happen? Their pitcher had given up one hit in the entire game so far. Our coach randomly pinch-hit someone—a rookie. And she hit a single over the second baseman's head. Our runner at second scored. She wasn't even a starting player. She came off the bench and had this epic moment as a rookie. We sent the runner home, and the score became 2–1. We had a runner at first base. They bunted her to second base. And there was a strikeout. So now there were two outs with one on second. Our number-nine hitter, also our catcher, was up to bat. I was back there holding my head going, "Aaahhh! We scored one, but we'll never score two!" And there were two strikes. This girl had struck out this entire time. The count was one ball and two strikes. She swung at this pitch—I don't know how she hit it. And she ended up hitting a walk-off home run—a home run that ended the game—over left center field. We dogpiled at home plate. To this day, I get chills telling this story. This is probably one of my favorite games ever. To this day it is this historic game within the Japan Softball League that everyone knows and talks about, because it was unheard of—Abbott versus Ueno. It was unheard of that I would miss the throw and that Ueno would give up three runs when they were up by so much. And one of them was a home run.

The president of Toyota was at the game. At this point, he had this "never give up" mentality that followed us throughout our careers. This emotional experience made him, and a lot of the fans, really fall in love with Toyota softball. He also became one of the main drivers who helped softball get back into the Olympics in 2020. Toyota was one of the top organizers of the 2020 Olympic Games.

The next year, 2011, we came back. The president had updated our entire softball field for us because we won. We got new dugouts. We got new turf in the outfield. And he gave us a team bus. It's actually really cute—it has little cartoon characters of all the players on it. There is a cartoon character of him on the bus, too. We won the championship again.

In 2012, we three-peated, winning our third consecutive championship—a first in the history of the Japan Softball League. We just kept growing, evolving, and getting better. In 2013 Yukkiko Ueno's team ended up winning on a Japanese hit-and-run play. And then we won again. The next year, we played

okunouchi_club

Thank you
@monicaabbott

なんて脚が長いんだ 💧

Monica pitched 14 successful
seasons for the Red Terriers
in Tokyo. Here, Monica
autographs a ball for a
fan as she prepares for a
professional softball game
with her Toyota Terrier team
at their home field.

them again and played extra, extra, extra innings. From then on, we would win; then they would win; then we would win, and it went on like that—up until 2019. All of those games were Abbott versus Ueno, and they were epic. They were games you would want to watch. There was so much drama and action and fun. It was better than reality TV.

After 2018, the league started to change. Toyota got some younger players—mostly pitchers—between 2019 and 2021. Technology has also improved. It is easier to be overseas—we can FaceTime and text people. There is Netflix, Hulu, and Amazon. When I first went to Japan, it wasn't like that. We were just entertaining ourselves. I feel like I had to grow up and figure things out. It is a lot easier now. They don't just bring pitchers and catchers over now, either; they bring the other defensive players, too, so we created a market for that. It is more common for a foreigner to throw to a Japanese catcher, which I think is really cool, because now Japanese catchers want to catch foreign pitchers. When I first came to Japan, maybe one or two left-handed pitchers were in the league, and now *every* team has one or two left-handed pitchers.

So, why did I go to Japan? When I first went abroad, that path wasn't highly accepted or known. People would be mad, asking, "Why do you go over there?" I responded, "They have over five thousand people at every game. For all of the big games, it is more like thirteen thousand. Why wouldn't I go over there?" Toyota draws really good fans. They love softball. They have cheerleaders and a band. It's because they have such good organization. The league is dependable. Japanese softball has been around for a while. They started in 1949 and have remained strong every year since the beginning. They treat me well, and I never have to worry if I am going to get paid. I never worry about what might happen if I get injured or if the accommodations will be bad. The level of play is exceptional. The competition is incredible. So, it's hard to say, "No." And I grow and get better.

They've just been top-notch and professional, and that wasn't always the case in the US. That's why I continued to play in Japan for so long. They appreciate me. Even in 2022, post-Olympics, I told them that I was not ready to retire, but that I didn't know whether I could play next season because I needed to start thinking about other parts of my life. I've been playing a ten-month season, all those sorts of things. I gave them a proposal saying I would play three weeks on, three weeks off. They came back and said they would rather have it this way, so I come at this date and leave early. I have a modified schedule compared to other athletes there this year. Obviously, they are doing that because I have been there so long. We have a good relationship. They don't do that for everyone. So, that is why I play in Japan, for Toyota. Not by choice. If I didn't have to play there, I wouldn't. But no pro team in the US is comparable to it. When I played in Japan and NPF, I was making a living playing full time. I actually got to play full time by playing in Japan and in the US, too.

Currently twenty-four teams are in the Japan Softball League, and the teams are owned by corporations. That makes it more of an activity for their company—the backer of the team. I play for Toyota Motor Corporation. I am a contracted athlete. Japanese Toyota players have responsibilities outside of the softball season. Some players work in an office. They do group projects. They do email, PR, etc. I have an office as well. Technically, I work for human resources.

"Monica is a pure competitor. The work she does behind the scenes and how much she puts into it are extraordinary. Her impact on the game is her work ethic and her pitching craft."

Natasha Watley, All American and US Olympic Infielder

I go there twice a season—once when I first get there, and then once before the finals to rally the troops.

There were US athletes who played in Japan before I did, but I would say that I brought the Japan league more to the forefront. More people recognized it as an option because of me. On the Japan side, they realized that more people wanted to come there. Now softball athletes see going to Japan as an opportunity or a goal—it is this coveted thing. All the teams in the States will work with you if you want to go there, because they realize the draw of the Japan League is not going to go away. It is a lot easier for people to go to Japan. Of course, there are challenges like the time change and the culture, but overall, the ability to live is easier.

Now it's a softball player's dream to play in Japan, and it's accepted. It has been a good experience for me. My career has been in Japan because there wasn't a full-time opportunity in the United States after college. I played in the NPF when the opportunities were there. I did everything I could to help the US grow. But Toyota gave me the opportunity to become more of a true professional. It is the weirdest thing; I know I don't speak the same language they do, but now my Japanese is decent enough to get by. I can't go to a deep level when it comes to speaking in Japanese. But even to this day, every time I leave, I cry. I feel sad. It is such a mutual investment—the team, the emotions, the feelings, with each other.

NINE GIRL IMPACT

Sports can help anyone, but especially girls, in significant ways. Sports gives them a positive place away from feeling down about whatever it is that is going on with their bodies. In high school I might have been thinking, "I feel so tall; the guy I like isn't as tall as I am; all my friends are super short; I am towering over everyone; I am huge—or whatever it is—my hair is frizzy; I don't look like the popular girl"—all of those things. You go to the softball field. You have two hours of practice. You have zero time to be thinking, "Wow, my hair is frizzy; I'm sweaty; I'd better not throw this girl out at first base." You don't have time to be worrying, "I'm taller than everyone on my team. Oh no! That means I won't get a hit today." You don't have time to worry about those trivial things. But I will say that when you put on a uniform, you do your hair for the game—I've worn a ribbon in my hair for most of my career. For a lot of my high school games, I wore these two French braids. All through high school, I always had some sort of braid in my hair, whether it was French braids or in my ponytail. Doing your hair, getting ready for the game, those sorts of things help give you confidence—it almost makes you feel like you are putting on your superhero outfit. You are putting on this attitude—this mental game—the way you want to feel in your heart. You are putting on courage. You are putting on confidence, a can-do attitude. To this day, I still try to have a braid somewhere in my hair because it is part of my identity as a pitcher—my own personal uniform. I wear my team's uniform, and the thing that makes me feel like I have this badge of honor, this courage, this mental strength, this strong heart—maybe it's the braid.

Sports helped guide me through some tough years when I could have gone down a different path. What is cool for those who excel in sports is that you are playing all your life,

> "Monica opened the nation's eyes to the game of softball."
>
> Julie Abbott,
> Monica's mother

Monica with a few Olympic hopefuls.

you go to high school, and all of a sudden you realize, "Oh my gosh! I may have an opportunity here. I may have a chance to make it." That is very motivating. It makes you want to work harder. In my case, there were people in my life who were really close to me who did take the wrong path and made some bad decisions. In some ways, they became my protectors, saying, "No, Monica! No, you can't do this. You are not coming. You are not allowed. Don't you have softball practice?" They were still my friends all through high school, but they knew that I could make it, that I had a chance to do something good. I think that is a true thing for a lot of people—you are guided, protected, and even sheltered by those around you because your sport can guide your opportunity. I didn't have time to do anything else.

Every time I lace up my cleats, I feel as if I am stepping into an alter ego. I just have this different sense of confidence, like a superhero. I really feel like it's my moment right before the game. I really do feel like sport ingrains it in you—the work ethic, the attitude. No one wants to hang out on the softball field or on a team with someone who has a bad attitude or is being lazy or is just negative. Everyone will tell you that they've had a bad day, and they'll come to practice feeling down—everyone has done it—being snippy or sassy because someone hurt their feelings or said something that made them up-set, or they are not feeling good about how they look today. Everybody experiences that. And people in sports will be the first ones to pick you up. They'll give you three minutes or five minutes to feel bad and talk about it, and then, "Okay, we are over it. Let's do what we are here to do now. Let's do something fun." That respect is really cool within a team. There are a lot of things on the softball field to celebrate.

Physical activity is essential for children and adults. The benefits are end-less. Analytical thinking improves with running, jumping, and throwing. We develop speed and power from physical activity. Sports gives emotional stability. During tough times, I went to the softball field. Even today playing softball or a workout really helps me think. Competition is healthy for kids as long as we are aware of tuning into their developmental stages. Learning how to lose is part of growing up. At the really young ages, I think it is important to ask, "Is your child having fun?" Is she asking you to go out and play catch? Is she asking you to run the bases? Is she smiling when she does it? Not every day has to be a good day, but are the majority of the days good days?

And then I would say don't feel that you need to rush kids into some-thing—into one-on-one coaching all the time. Don't feel like you need to rush them into pitching or hitting lessons or travel ball—let that develop naturally. If she wants to pitch, she is going to tell you. Even in the very be-ginning, I started later when I had more coordination. I had one pitching lesson a month for the first year. Don't rush things. Let your child develop her skills and athleticism and have fun with it.

As far as participation trophies and all of that, you want to teach your child competitiveness—to be competitive and to strive to do their best. The participation medals are needed at a certain level at very young ages—like T-ball. As they get older you want to teach them how to be competitive, and that means winning and losing. That points to focusing on things like most improved and best sportsmanship. Teach them how they get better and celebrate their wins on the field.

My grandma came to all of my games, and I would get so mad when we lost. One day she said to me, "Just because you lost does not mean you are not going to play a game again. You can't let everything affect your life and the people around you. Hey, you lost. She played better than you did today. There is nothing you can do about it. Did you give it your all today? Did you give it 100 percent? No? Well then you should be mad. Did you play with all your heart? Yes? Well then you are good. You left it all on the field."

My dad did a really good job of teaching me how to turn failure into a learning process. He would ask me questions. What was I thinking when I threw this pitch? When the shortstop made an error, what was my first thought? Dad would say, "Your face looked different after the throwing error; did you even have a plan? If you could do it again, what would you do differently? Why? What is the action?" I would be so mad, and my mom and my dad would give me the same love and attention after every game. I would still get a hug from them no matter what. Because the family was so big and so busy, to get this focused time with them at the game meant so much more.

I definitely feel like I had a mini tribe—especially my mom and dad. I remember saying, "Mom, I am old enough now, I could go with someone else. I could stay with someone else on the road. You could go to Gina and Bina's game if you want." My mom would say, "You don't want me to go, Monica?" I would say, "I want you to go. But if you have to go to their game, I understand." My mom was with me all the time. She drove to all the tournaments. And my grandma would go if we were within an hour or an hour and a half. There were eight adults in my life that stepped up—my mom and dad, my grandma and grandpa, Jean Ashen, Keith Berg, Kenny Gardner, and Darren Jackson.

I am against a child playing one sport from day one all the way through. It is actually becoming less popular,

> "In twenty-two years, I never coached anyone like Monica."
>
> Darren Jackson, basketball coach, North Salinas High School

and I actually started a scholarship, which is given out to female athletes. It requires the recipient to be a multi-sport athlete in high school. I think it is really beneficial to have the balance, whether you are highly competitive at both sports or just doing the other one for fun. It is important to have a balance of different athletic skills—just being a little more well-rounded and versatile, not only as an athlete but also as a person. It is good to prioritize which sport is your main focus, but having that well roundedness can prevent injuries, help round out your personality, and teach you other life skills. Participating in other sports can give you information and change you in positive ways. Looking at it now, basketball was a good complement to softball for me. Basketball is constantly intense. Softball has intense moments. In basketball, I played in the paint. That was rough and toughened me up. In softball, I pitch with a circle around me, the island or bubble that no one wants to come into. In basketball everyone was in my space; in softball everyone was out. I played softball and basketball throughout high school and thought about playing volleyball and track and field. I was in a bunch of clubs, but time was limited. I knew my priority was softball. By your junior year in high school, you should know which sport is your priority.

Growing up, I didn't really know what Title IX was. When I was in high school, my athletics director had a national girls and women in sports day. I think I was a freshman. I went to the workshop, and they told us about Title IX. My high school athletics director said, "Yes, I played basketball in that era in college. We played six-on-six basketball with teams of three forwards and three guards. Only the forwards could shoot the ball. The forwards and guards had to stay on their sides of the court." My mom played softball growing up, and she told me about it, too. As I moved forward, I realized, "Wow, this is really a big deal. I never heard about this."

When you are growing up, you don't think about gender. When I was ten years old, I never once thought that I couldn't become a professional softball player. My brother could be a professional ball player, so I could, too. You don't think about that separation when you are young—you have no concept of it. It didn't really hit me until high school and then going into college at Tennessee. I loved the fact that Tennessee had a men's department and a women's department.* That totally made sense to me.

I didn't realize the impact of all of this right away. Now, my mind is blown by it. Softball was really growing. There is a Women's Sports Foundation. Billie Jean King was named Sportsperson of the Year in 1972 by *Sports Illustrated*. When I was right out of college, I got to go up there and learn so much about all of it. It was such a big deal. It was a natural transition for me to become an advocate for women and women's sports. It fell naturally into the things I was already doing and who I am as a person—how I grew up. I grew up with strong women in my family. My mom was strong. Every pitcher would say, "My dad is my catcher." And I would always say with pride," Well, my mom is my catcher." I grew up around very athletic and strong women. They were go-getters. They weren't afraid to create something if it needed to be created. Going to Tennessee, playing professionally for Japan, and running my business, Abbott Athletics—it has all made sense and fallen into place because it was naturally ingrained in me by the people around me and the people I grew up with. And then seeing it in Pat Summitt, in what Jennie Finch and Jessica Mendoza were able to do, seeing Billie Jean King and some of the other famous women—that just magnified everything.

I think as we get older, perspectives change, and we realize other ways that sports become more important to females or just athletes in general. Mental toughness, mental strength, and mental stability are definite outcomes of sports. I think everyone is emotional, but women—we really feel our emotions a lot more. I think sports gives us that emotional stability to be able to handle all those different feelings. A team sport gives us a common bond with the emotions, so we don't always feel that we are going through them alone. I would also say that during tough times and during good times, sports give

---

*In 2011 the University of Tennessee men's and women's athletics departments merged into one.

you an escape. During some of the toughest moments of my life, I went to the softball field. I went and practiced to clear my mind—to clear everything out to get back to what I could do—to what I could and couldn't control.

People ask me what it's like to break barriers and to be a role model. I feel good about it. I hope I am doing a good job. I hope that I can do a good job and be worthy of someone looking up to me or wanting to be like me. I hope that it is not just because I can throw seventy-five mph, but because of all the things that that encompasses. It is an honor. It sounds like such a cliché, but a lot of women have to see something before they can do it. It is hard to dream dreams and have role models in things that haven't been done before.

If I can be the person who does it so that someone coming after me can do it, too, how cool is that? Watching the younger generation and seeing young people coming up, I see it everywhere now. I was the first one to do it—to pitch like that. And people made fun of me or looked at me as "funky." They were always asking me, "Why are you bending over? Why do you pitch like that? What's it for? What's it doing? Why would you do something like that?" Well, I've got to own this. This is my style. This is what I do. All these years later, I can see that there are many pitchers that I have impacted, because now I can see them having a low position start or creating momentum off of the mound. I can see I have also impacted people that don't pitch this way, like Montana Fouts at Alabama, another really tall pitcher, creating hip angle and throwing the ball hard—and being proud of that. That is a big thing. That wasn't the case back in the day. I can see those things. You can see the more dynamic pitchers out there, like Megan Faraimo. And I think, "Oh, my gosh! I can tell I have totally influenced this girl. I influenced her. Oh, my gosh! She liked me when she was 12." I answer all my messages and sign all the autographs that I can for people. I do what I can to really give them a special moment, because that stuff is important. I try to be a light for them.

I think people throw the term "role model" around loosely. It's like the word "GOAT." You can't call a college player a GOAT. To be designated the "greatest of all time," an athlete needs to be battle-tested and show longevity. In the same way, "role model" is a title that needs to be earned. It is earned through action, not necessarily through play, but it can include both. It's not easy, because there are some days you don't want to be out there. You are having a bad day, or things didn't go right in the game, or you are tired. Whatever it is, people expect you to turn it on for them when they don't realize that being a role model is not an obligation.

It's easy to preach the women's side, and I know that will go well. But I do think the longer I look at it, the longer I am in the game, the more I realize how much of an impact I've had on the male audience as well. So many of them started watching softball when I played, and they fell in love with the sport. A lot of boys come to games now, and it's cool that it's exciting to them and that they recognize me. In Japan, I get stopped by more young boys than I do young girls around the little Toyota City area. They have boys' softball in Japan as well. They have men's baseball players and men's softball players, but I get stopped by more young baseball players than girls. I stand out more, and they know me, and they say, "Wow, we watched you! We were at the game!" A lot of them are just more avid fans—willing to share—whereas women are a little bit more hesitant to say "I watched" or are shy for no reason.

In the future I'm hoping more and more women become softball stars. Every year we see more women able to make a living playing. Right now, women have to make a living doing a lot of different jobs as an athlete. I think as each generation passes, we'll see fewer doing ten different jobs; we'll see less need for additional jobs and more substantial income with softball. We definitely need a better professional system, like an east and west or a north and south league—slowly building it up that way to assure some long-term playing opportunity for these athletes. When I first started playing pro, most people stopped playing softball when they were twenty-five, unless they were an Olympian. If they were an Olympian, they would play into their thirties. Now, a good group of people are playing into their late twenties. A handful of us are playing into our mid-thirties.

I have had a lot of good opportunities. If anything, I just hope that one day, softball players can get a shoe named after them that lasts for a long time. Today a softball player cannot get a lifetime glove deal. But maybe one day, we'll have a movie based on a softball star's life. That is where the sport is going. It is scary sometimes to be the first athlete carrying the torch. It's also scary to be the one investing in that person to make it last long-term.

Think about the athletic stars you know. The only reason these people are household names is because they are covered by the media. They are on prime-time TV, and companies invest marketing dollars in them. I don't want to say they are not good athletes or don't deserve it, because they have fought a long battle to get up there, too. If you take it down a level to triple-A or double-A minor league baseball, where is the comparison? Part of it is the notoriety of being on TV—being publicized, being covered in the media. The list goes on and on. We should be getting equal sponsorships. Thanks to streaming technology, now softball and women's sports are getting more coverage, but it is still not the same.

College athletes sign NIL (name, image, and likeness) deals now. This NCAA policy was designed for the men's basketball and football stars—maybe women's basketball stars to an extent, and people who become famous on TikTok or Instagram in high school. Now these athletes are in college to continue their business. This policy might end up having momentum like Title IX: it is going to create many female athletes who are going to make a lot of money and get endorsements in college. The big question we are going to have to answer is, will the endorsements and name and brand recognition follow those female athletes after college to the professional side? College athletes will come into these professional leagues with expectations and standards that will hold the leagues accountable to paying a certain amount of money and to letting athletes bring their sponsors with them.

Now as an adult softball player and a longtime professional, I can see how doors just opened for me. I just kept running through doors. When I see there's a chance for me, I take it and run with it as far as I can. But I also think about how now, I need to open doors for other people. I think about all the people who opened doors for me and enabled me to run through them. But how can I open a door for someone else? How can I open a door for a team or an organization or a group to really help them jump a level in whatever it is they are doing?

There are a million different ways to open doors for people—to empower them. It doesn't always have to be money. It can be being excited about something. It can be teaching something small—showing them how to create game plans. It can be teaching something big to bring about success, putting on an event, negotiating, branding, and putting other people in a position to be the hero. When you can think about creating those opportunities for people, it is really impactful. It changes people's lives and perspectives on things.

As far as my career success, I give credit to my dad. When I first went to Japan, we didn't know how long it was going to last. I was making good money for playing softball, but it could have lasted just one year—the contracts go year to year—or it could have lasted five years; we just had no idea. Dad helped me start an event camps and clinics business. We figured out how to brand, how to give a good speech, how to organize the events—all of those things we needed to get it started. We launched a little store with merchandise. My dad was the moving factor behind that, and it really helped me become a softball person fulltime. I think my dad had good business sense. I think my grandpa had suggested it, too. I had to do something. I had an opportunity. What was the best way to capitalize on it? I knew right out of college that I could do a clinic, because I had done some in Knoxville. I had given a couple of lessons in college on the side. I knew that I could educate in softball, sport, and life. Where dad came in was to help legitimize my business. This was all before social media, and we started small. We started marketing with my rec league, my travel ball league, and my neighborhood. Both Olympic years, I actually made more money from endorsements and events than I did from playing US softball. I stepped through doors toward new possibilities that kept me in the softball world—my passion. To this day, I am living my dream.

As for my own future? I will always be involved in softball somehow. I may not be playing years down the road, but I am always going to be an advocate for—and an expert in—the sport of softball. I want to see the next Monica Abbott. I want to see her throw eighty miles an hour and sign a $5 million contract and get a shoe deal or a glove deal that lasts long after she is playing. It doesn't have to end.

APPENDIX 1 ABBOTT'S A-LIST

HOW TO BRING IT ON AND OFF THE FIELD

Dear Reader,

Softball has had a huge impact on my life! Honestly, sometimes I sit back
and wonder, How did a 6'3" lefty end up in softball and not basketball or
volleyball or tennis or swimming? Why softball? The truth is, I fell in love
with the game, and over time with some consistent practice and effort
I started to get good, and that made me like it even more.

As I get close to ending my playing career, I can see that some themes
have been constant throughout my life, whether it was in recreation softball
with my family, club softball as I laid my heart on my sleeve or professionally as I was challenged to constantly evolve and grow. Playing softball has
been a big part of my life, and I am so blessed to have had the opportunity to grow up and grow through the sport. As I look back and as I look
forward, I notice some themes that have been a big part of my career as an
athlete and as a woman in sport.

I wrote "Abbott's A-List" with this in mind. It's a place to dream, find
advice, share your challenges, and build the confidence you need in any
arena that calls your name. I have learned much along the way to reaching
my dreams, and I am eternally grateful. Thank you for being on this journey
with me, and I hope that this list will give you the strength you need to help
you reach your biggest dream.

Monica Abbott #MA14

Abbott's A-List

1   **Set goals early to reach your dreams.**
The bigger you dream, the harder it can seem for you to believe it will come true. Here is what to do: Break it down to a process—make a series of steps to help you achieve them. This can help you make your dream come true.

2   **Remember to play.**
Softball is a game. It's a game—you are supposed to play with energy, and with a smile. Yes, it has its ups and downs. But it is a game, and games are meant to be played! So, play with childlike joy.

3   **Be proactive.**
Take the initiative. Seriously. Be proactive. No one is going to come to you and hold your hand and take you to practice. So, be the person that makes it happen and create the future you want.

4   **Develop a routine.**
A solid routine will help create confidence for you. When things go bad, have a routine. Yes, seriously, have a routine for when things go bad . . . I know it may sound like a joke. :) But having something small that can reset you back into your normal routine is essential to success.

5   **Be great at something.**
I am here to tell you, don't be afraid to be great at something. I challenge you: Instead of going for a bunch of good things, take that good thing, invest in it, and make it great. Go be great at it, every day.

6   It takes a team.

Look at the people around you right now who are helping you. Family, coaches, friends, teachers, support staff . . . I bet there are quite a few people you can think of. It takes a team and a community of people to help support you, to make you blossom and grow. So, bring them along your journey.

7   Loyalty matters.

Loyalty brings out character. It leads to true thought and conversation that will bring out that tough love component that is so important to your growth in all aspects of life. And that starts with loyalty.

8   Let go.

Play free. Thinking is for practice! Stop thinking so hard. And let go. Let go of all the distractions and all the things that you carry with you between the white lines. Let go to grow.

9   Reinvent yourself.

There are a lot of different ways to be successful on the field. Different styles and signatures of play that can help you excel. You never find that out unless you reinvent your game or the way you think about the game. Yes, it is risky because it is scary. Growing can be scary, but seeing growth is awesome. That's why it's so important to constantly rethink and reinvent yourself. It's worth it.

10   Celebrate the good!

Think about how many wins it takes to get to a loss. Think about how many little wins it takes to get a big win. Don't underestimate celebrating the good daily. Celebrate the daily wins. Little wins daily are powerful for the big moment. For the big win!

11   Be all in.

If you are going to do something, you might as well do it right. If you are going to take the time, be all in for it. And don't just be all in for yourself, be all in for the people that are working with you—for your team, for those surrounding you, do what it takes.

12   Have short-term memory loss.

Don't carry the bad things that happen with you. Leave them in the past. Even if they just happened, there is a reason they happened and now as of this very moment they are in the past. Just leave them there. Look forward and be mature enough to take the good parts from it and be ready to apply them as you make the next memory.

13   Invest in your sport.

This is the Monica Abbott challenge. Anybody who is reading this, if you are a woman in your sport: give back to it. Don't just be satisfied by saying you are a mentor; do more. Think. How can you actually have an impact?

14   Follow your heart.

My grandma always said this to me. It is so true: Just follow your heart; let your heart guide you. You will know when it is right and when it is wrong. And most importantly, don't be afraid to listen your heart. It is about the things that make your heart beat—things that make you feel alive. The things you do that make you feel excited every morning or every afternoon before you step onto the field for practice.

APPENDIX 2 CAREER HIGHLIGHTS

Six-time Japan Softball League Champion (2010, 2011, 2012, 2014, 2016, 2018)

Five-time Japan Softball League MVP (2010, 2011, 2012, 2016, 2018)

Two-time USA Olympic Silver Medalist (2008, 2021)

All-Olympic Team Member (2021)

Pitched first perfect game in Olympic history (2008)

Four-time World Champion Gold Medalist (2006, 2010, 2018, 2022)

Two-time Pan American Gold Medalist (2007, 2019)

World Games Gold Medalist (2022)

Five-time National Pro Fastpitch Champion (2007, 2011, 2013, 2015, 2017)

Four-time NPF MVP (2007, 2011, 2015, 2017)

Five-time NPF Pitcher of the Year (2011, 2012, 2015, 2016, 2017)

Nine-time All-NPF Selection (2009, 2010, 2011, 2012, 2013, 2014, 2015, 2016, 2017)

Women's Sports Foundation Sportswoman of the Year (2007)

Honda Award Winner in Softball (2007)

Four-time All-American, University of Tennessee (2004–7)